A VOYAGE IN A DORY
From Sitka to Tacoma
by Oars, Sail and Tow Rope

by R.N. DeArmond

Photographs by the author

Arrowhead Press
112 Barracks Street
Sitka, Alaska 99835

1999

i

Also by R.N. DeArmond

- Some Names Around Juneau (place names)
- The Founding of Juneau
- Old Gold, Historical Vignettes of Juneau
- Nine Early Visitors to Southeastern Alaska
- Who's Who in Alaska Politics, with Evangeline Atwood
- Lady Franklin Visits Sitka (editor)
- Raven Town, with Dale DeArmond
- The True Story of the Discovery of Gold
  on Bonanza Creek, with Dale DeArmond
- Tales of a Klondike Newsman (editor)
- Klondike Newsman, Stroller White (editor)
- Names on the Chart
- A Chronology of Sitka
- From Sitka's Past
- The USS SAGINAW in Alaska Waters, 1868-1869
- Baranof Island's Eastern Shore, with Patricia Roppel
- Belinda Mulrooney, a Biography, with Melanie J. Mayer
  (at the publisher; title subject to change)

ISBN 1-929292-00-7
Library of Congress Catalog Card Number 99-63925

Cover design and layout by Marianne Thomson

For

Laurie Bruce Johnson

A caring nurse, a good friend and
an enthusiastic boatwoman. Her interest
and urging prompted me to put this
story on paper.

Author's Foreword

When I left Sitka in a 16-foot dory bound for Tacoma, Washington, I had no thought of writing a book about the trip. And the idea did not occur to me during the next 66 years. I did record a lot of details of the trip with the portable typewriter I took along, but it turned out that much of the record was not permanent. I wrote to my parents whenever there was a place to mail a letter, eleven in all. Much more frequently I wrote to a school teacher I had been going with in Sitka and those letters had a lot more detail about the landscape I passed, the places where I stopped and the people I met and visited with. She and I had no commitments and while I was at college following the trip she married a logger and burned all my letters. That didn't bother me until 66 years later when I began to write this book. Then I wished that I had them back.

I did keep a log, fairly complete on some days; very incomplete on others, depending upon the weather and how tired I was at the end of the day. And my mother had kept all of my letters and returned them to me. The log book and the letters survived several moves, but the charts I had used, and on which I had marked exactly the places I stopped and other information, are long gone. Also badly faded if not gone are memories of some parts of the journey.

In the spring of 1998 Ken Fate of Raven Radio asked for an interview about the trip and I refreshed my memory with the log book and letters. One person who heard the interview urged me to write the story, as is indicated in the dedication. I was reluctant, but tackled it, and what you have here is the result. Some of the pictures I took had survived and are reproduced with the text.

With one exception I believe the story is accurate as to times, places and events. After a recent study of the charts of the West Coast, however, I believe the stranding behind a highwater island took place farther south than I have it in the story, off Sukkwan Island rather than Tuxekan Island.

Contents

Maps follow this page

Photographs

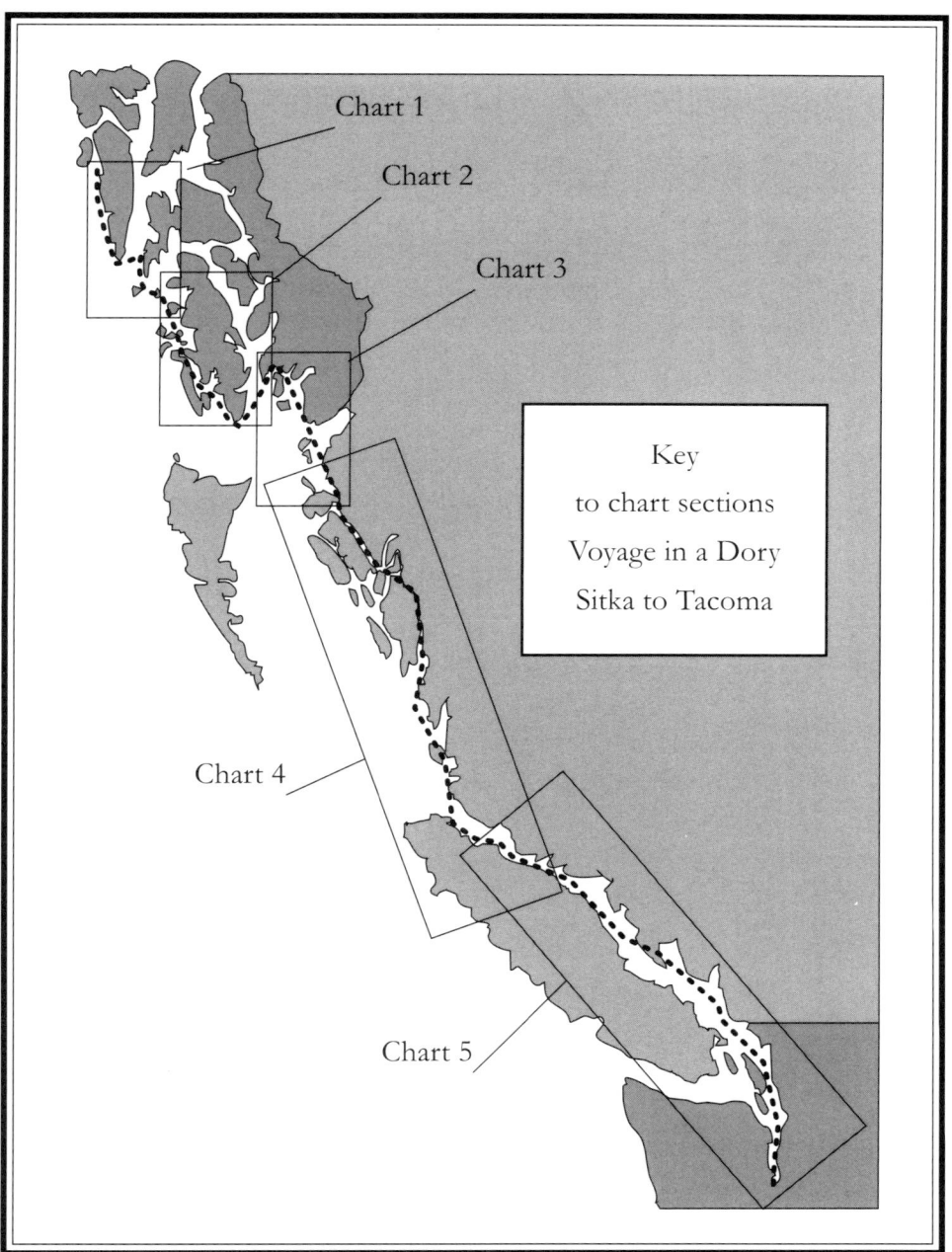

Chart 1

Chart 2

Chart 3

Key
to chart sections
Voyage in a Dory
Sitka to Tacoma

Chart 4

Chart 5

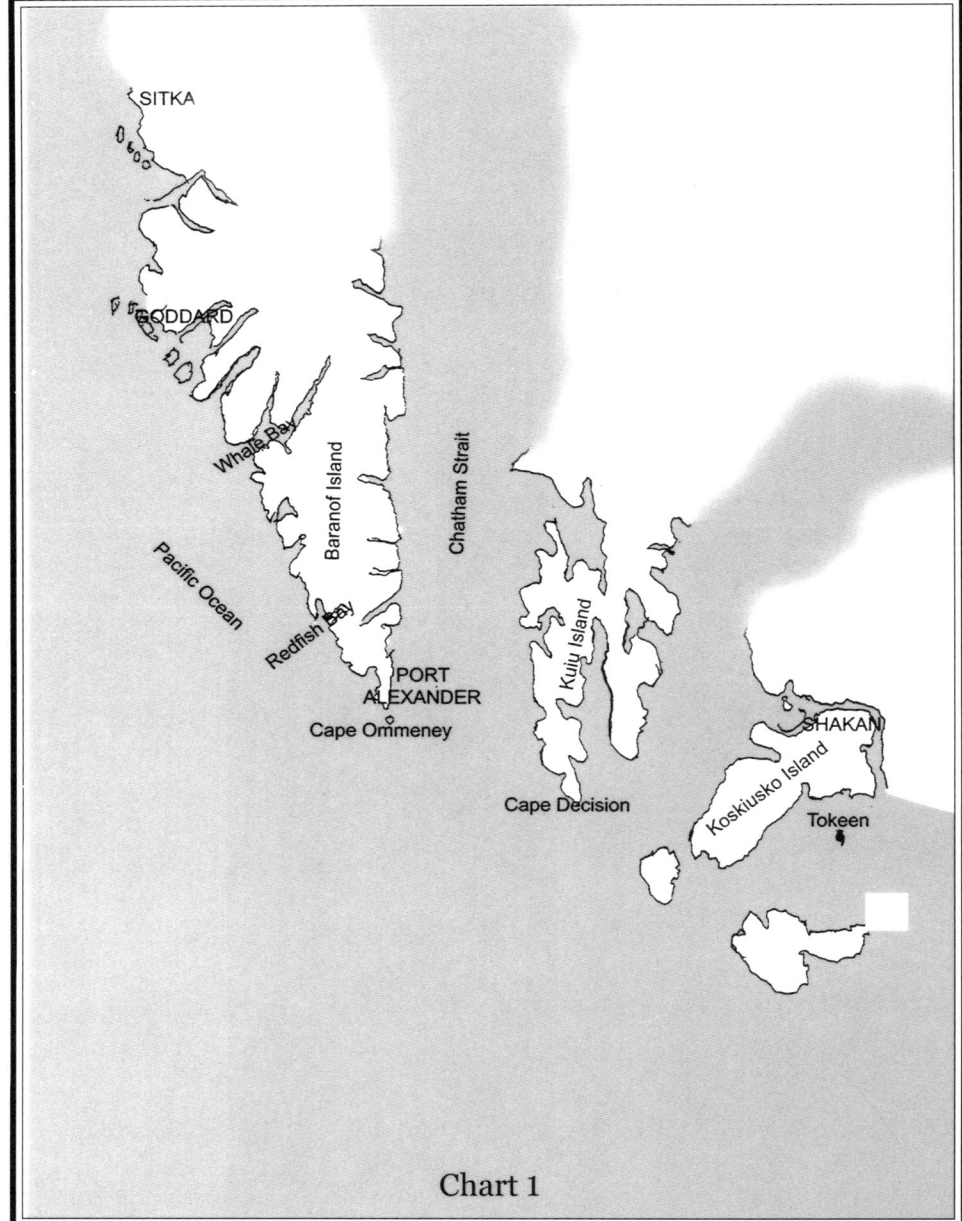

SITKA

GODDARD

Whale Bay

Baranof Island

Chatham Strait

Pacific Ocean

Redfish Bay

PORT ALEXANDER

Cape Ommeney

Kuiu Island

Cape Decision

SHAKAN

Koskiusko Island

Tokeen

Chart 1

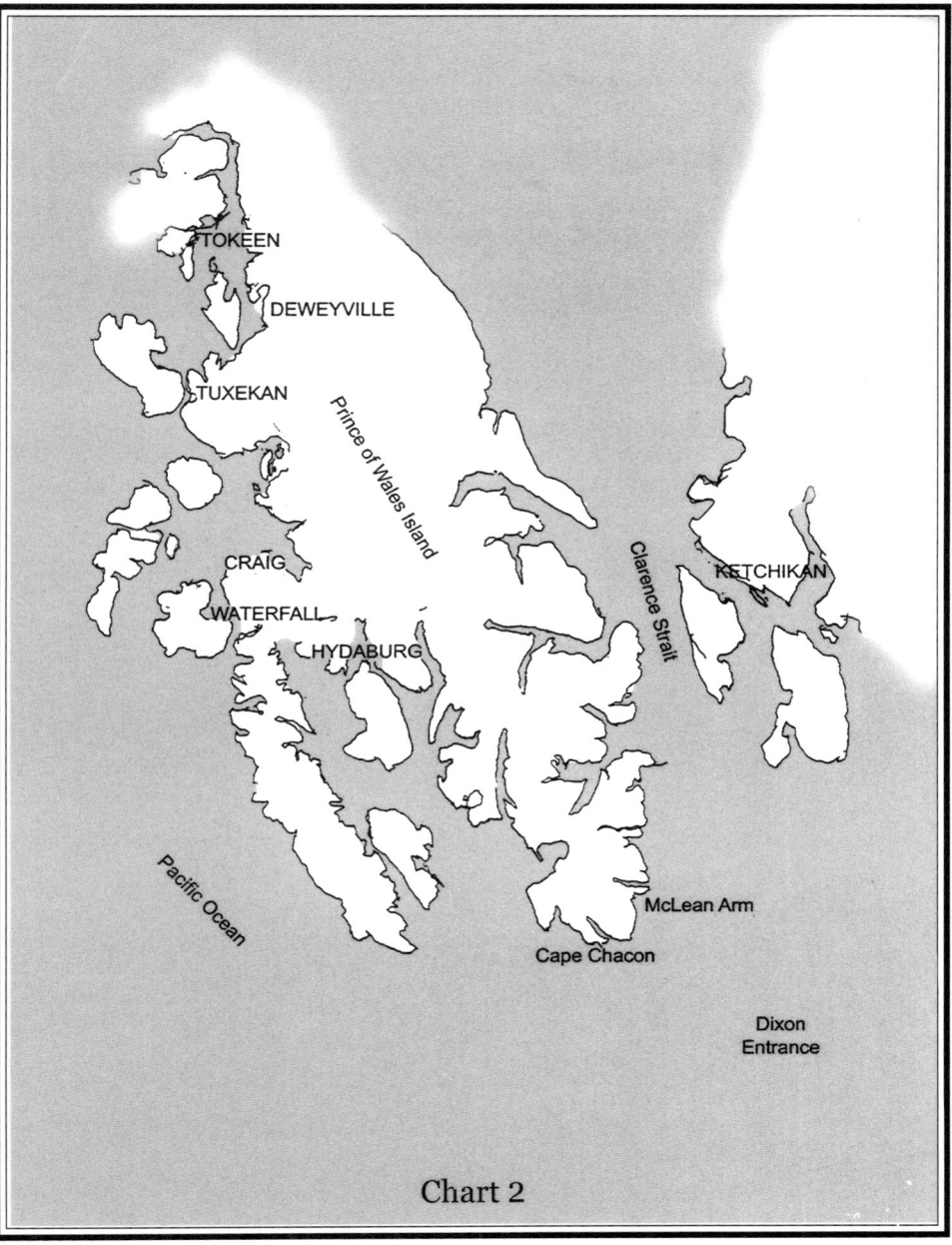

TOKEEN

DEWEYVILLE

TUXEKAN

Prince of Wales Island

CRAIG

WATERFALL

HYDABURG

KETCHIKAN

Clarence Strait

Pacific Ocean

McLean Arm

Cape Chacon

Dixon
Entrance

Chart 2

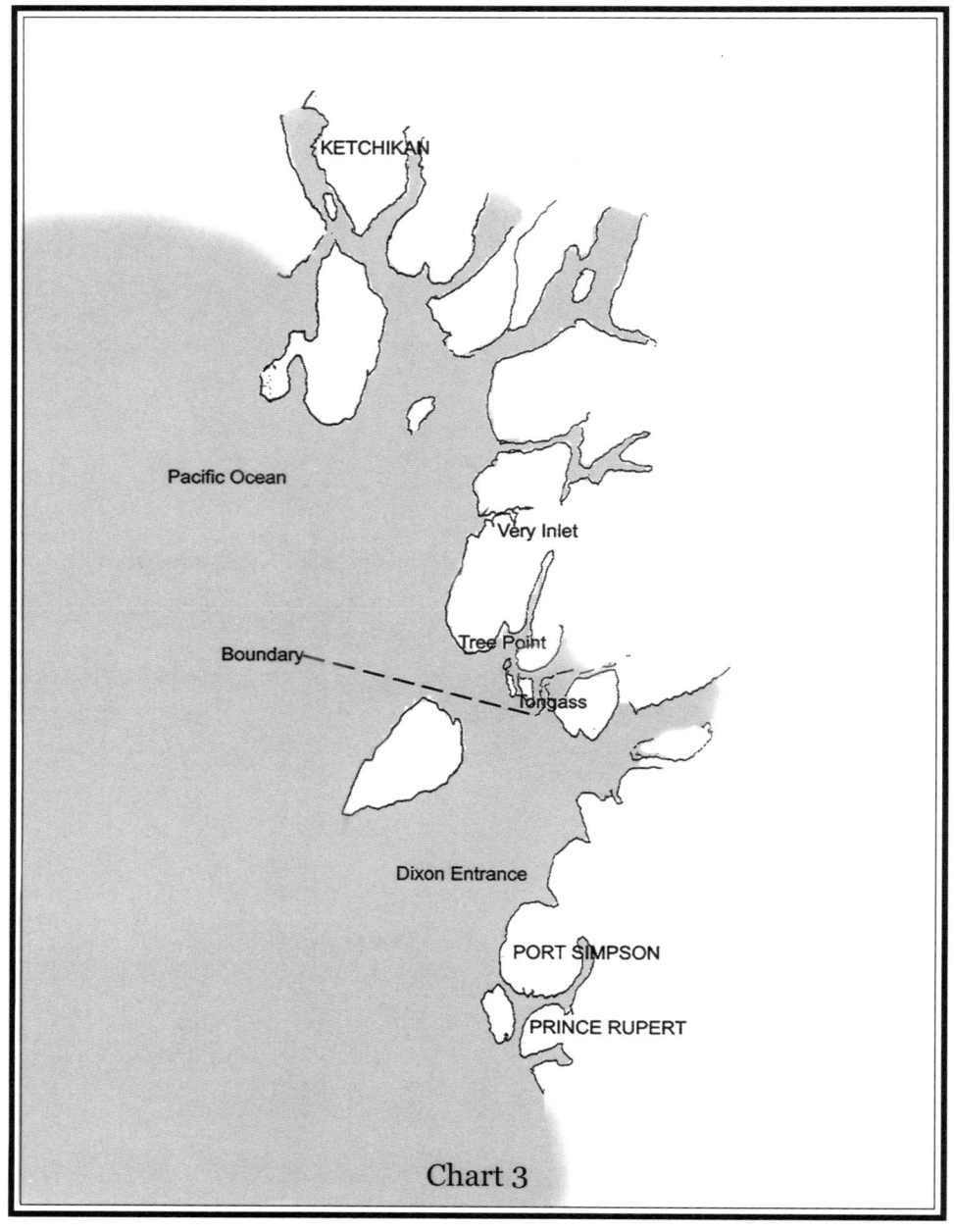

KETCHIKAN

Pacific Ocean

Very Inlet

Tree Point

Boundary

Tongass

Dixon Entrance

PORT SIMPSON

PRINCE RUPERT

Chart 3

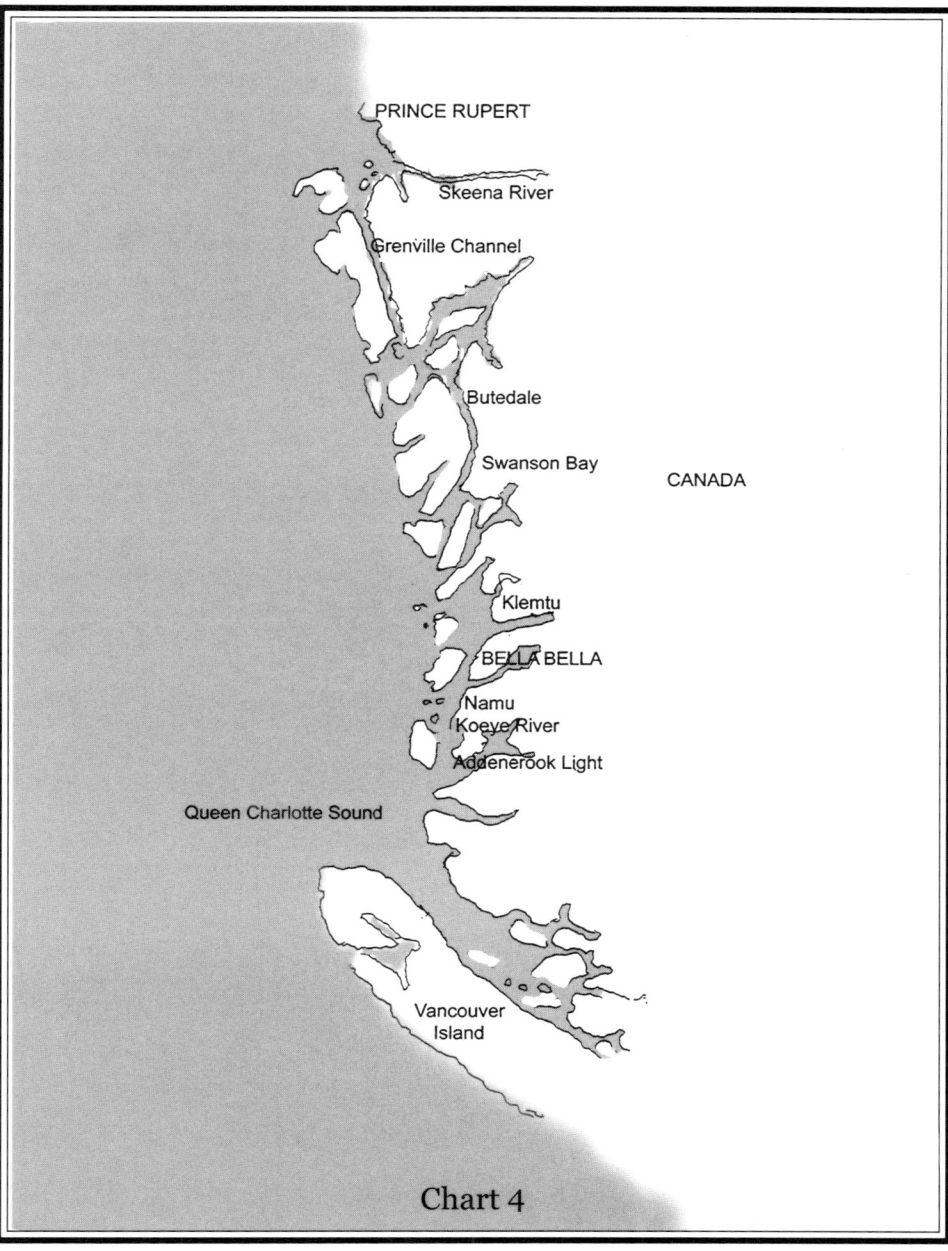

PRINCE RUPERT

Skeena River

Grenville Channel

Butedale

Swanson Bay

CANADA

Klemtu

BELLA BELLA

Namu

Koeye River

Addenerook Light

Queen Charlotte Sound

Vancouver
Island

Chart 4

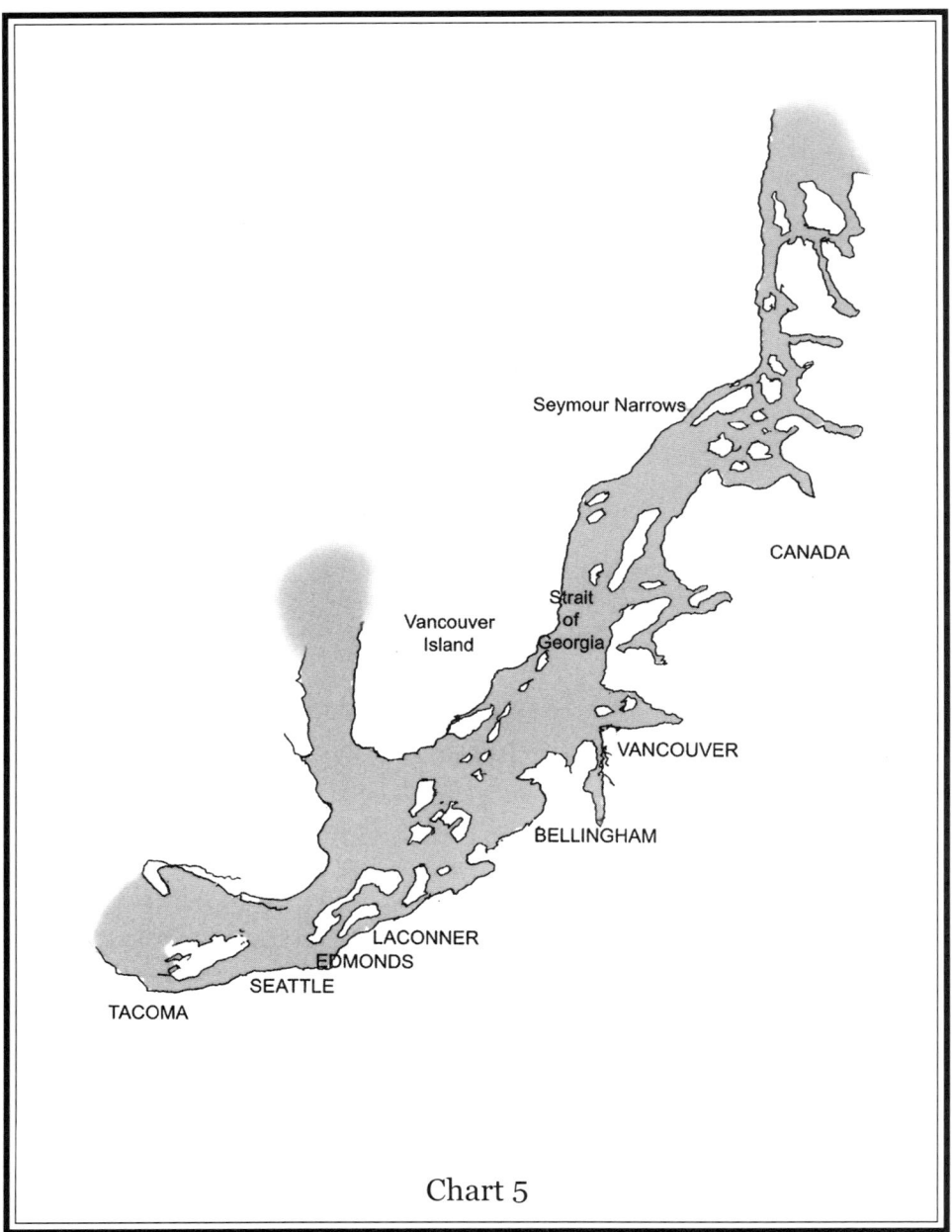

Chart 5

A VOYAGE IN A DORY
Sitka to Tacoma by Oars, Sail and Tow Rope

Why the Dory Trip?

The short answer is that I wanted to see more of the great Inside Passage that extends from the south end of Puget Sound in Washington State to the north end of Lynn Canal in Southeastern Alaska. I was born in Sitka, Alaska, at the end of July in 1911. About the time I was a year old my mother took me with her to visit her parents in Tacoma. My sister Ruth was born in Tacoma during that visit and returned with us to Sitka. Thereafter and until 1918, when both my grandparents died, we made several trips to Tacoma. And in the 1920s I made several round trips, one to receive medical attention, three to attend high school. But all of those trips were on steamboats, of various sizes and house flags. They usually did not make stops south of Ketchikan and they passed many places that I wanted to see more closely.

I graduated from Stadium High School in Tacoma in June 1930, and did not wait for the commencement exercises but returned home to Sitka by the first available steamer, which happened to be the ALAMEDA of the Alaska Steamship Company. During the stop at Juneau I approached E.J. "Stroller" White of Stroller's Weekly for a job as reporter. I told him I wanted to work for a year before going to college. He suggested that I find a summer job in Sitka, which would probably pay more than he could afford, and write to him in the fall. He did not promise a job, but I took his advice. I worked for a part of the summer at the Pyramid Packing Company cannery. Most of my work was in the can loft where the No. 1 tall cans that had been collapsed for shipment were re-formed and bottoms put on them, ready to be filled with salmon. At the end of the canning season, in August, I went trolling with a man named Sam Butts in his boat, the SKATE.

We went from Sitka to what was then known to the fishermen as the Gunk Hole, a name imported from the East Coast by an old cod fisherman named Buck Larry and which designated a safe and secure harbor. The name was later changed to the more elegant-sounding Elfin Cove. The establishment at the Gunk Hole consisted of two house scows owned by Ernest O. Swanson, a fish buyer and mild cure operator. One scow was used for the fish buying and processing, the other was the living quarters for Ernie Swanson and his fish splitter and salter, Donald Hanebury. In that scow there was also a small supply of staples for sale to the fishermen.

We fished and picked strawberries and did some hunting and some prospecting until after the first of October. We then ran to Hoonah and I caught the mail boat ESTEBETH back to Sitka. I had not much more than reached home than news was received of the death of Stroller White. I wrote to a couple of other papers but by then the Depression was getting into full stride and jobs were scarcer than ever. Then I learned that Stroller's widow, Mrs. Josephine White, was going to continue to operate the weekly paper and I wrote to her. About the end of the year she wired me that she had an opening. So I went to Juneau.

I had an interesting five months in Juneau as the only reporter on a weekly newspaper. That was the year the present Capitol building was first occupied, and the tenth Territorial Legislature went into its 60-day session there in March, with a bunch of old-time Alaskans among its 24 members. But that is another story. In May Mrs. White sold Stroller's Weekly to Hal Selby, a longtime Alaska newspaperman. He planned to fill his columns with clips from the exchanges and did not need a reporter. So I was out of a job.

I flew back to Sitka, my first plane ride. The job market was dismal in Sitka. The Pyramid Packing Company cannery was not going to operate that year. The trolling fleet was on strike and the halibut price was at rock bottom and few deliveries were being made at the Sitka Cold Storage. I had always enjoyed rowing, I was planning to attend the University of Oregon that fall, and with little prospect of summer work in Sitka it seemed a good time for a rowboat trip to Puget Sound.

The idea was by no means novel. Jack and Sasha Calvin had paddled a canoe from Puget Sound to Juneau three years earlier and I knew that many of the handtrollers back in the years before motors replaced oars had made the trip frequently. I looked around for a suitable rowboat, preferably a round bottomed double-ender about 16 feet long, but didn't find one.

There wasn't time to have that kind of boat built so I went to Andrew Hope and Arthur "Scotty" Jennings, who were operating a boat shop, and asked them to build me a dory. I had never used a dory but I knew that they were both seaworthy and fast to build. Andrew and Scotty didn't have plans for a dory but they went aboard a halibut schooner that was in port, measured its 19-foot dory and scaled it back to 16 feet. In a few days they turned out a well built boat and the cost was $50, a price that seems incredible in 1998.

The dory was cranky, as probably all dories are when light, but I found that I could sit on the gunwale without it capsizing. And I did not travel light.

The boat gear included two pair of spruce oars, a short mast that could be unstepped, a loose-footed sprit sail, a halibut anchor with 12 feet of chain and a hundred feet of line, and an extra coil of a hundred feet of buoy line. The painter was one-inch line and twice the length of the boat and was spliced into the bow. The end could be bent to a becket spliced into the stern, forming a sling for hoisting the boat out of water.

Other gear included a 7x7 wall tent of waterproof canvas, a long tarpaulin that covered the boat from end to end, an air mattress and a couple of wool blankets, a two-burner gasoline stove, a five-gallon keg for water, a kerosene lantern, a water-tight box that held a portable typewriter and a camera that took postcard size pictures, and other odds and ends, and another box to hold foodstuffs that needed to be kept dry. And I left Sitka with a far larger assortment of food, most of it in tin, than was really needed.

The dory, in other words, was loaded.

Sitka to Tokeen

It was 10:30 on a sunny Tuesday morning, June 22, 1931, when I pulled away from the Standard Oil Company float in Sitka, waved good-bye to my parents and a sister, and headed out through the islands toward Goddard Hot Springs. I went through the hole behind the rocks at Cape Burunof and through Pihl's Hole. There was a very light westerly breeze but not enough to be worth putting up the sail.

In Pihl's Hole I stopped to peel and eat an orange and near the boat I saw a little diving duck and a small black bass. At first I thought they were fighting and that perhaps the fish had attacked the duck. I could see them plainly against the clamshell bottom and after I watched for a bit I concluded that they were playing. The duck came to the surface for air now and again and could easily have flown away if it believed itself in danger. But it didn't fly and dove again to find its playmate. They were still at it when I pulled away.

A short way beyond Pihl's Hole I passed the Taigud Islands where J.H. "Banny" Banvard and his wife Kate were operating a fox farm for the Conga Fox Farm Company. The principal stockholder was her father, John H. Peterson, a Sitka merchant. Banny had come to Sitka as a radio operator at the Naval Radio Station on Japonski Island, a stone's throw from Sitka. He married Kate and when he retired from the service they decided to stay in Sitka, and that was about the time fox farming started in the area. He and Kate had a small gasboat with which he trolled for salmon and with which they also fished for black bass and other rockfish for fox feed. The main island had been used, several years earlier, for a fox farm scene in the movie "Rocking Moon" which was based on a book by Alaska writer Barrett Willoughby. Thereafter the island became known locally as Rocking Moon Island, but the name never got on the charts. Perhaps I would have stopped for a visit had their boat been at anchor in front of the house, but it wasn't and I moved on.

I was a mile or so from the Hot Springs when Al Lindegarde and his wife came along in their boat and offered me a tow, but I waved them off. Later in the trip I would have taken the tow. It was 8:30 when I tied up at the Goddard float. The Goddards' boat, the EDM, was there and so was Fred "Yakima Kid" Wolleson's troller. Fred, a highliner troller, was born in Washington State but not in Yakima. The first boat he bought was named Yakima and he retained it for the boat and acquired it for himself.

The reason Fred was tied up at the Springs was that the Territory of Alaska had established a school there to serve the children of the fox farmers on the nearby islands, and the schoolteacher was young and comely. Her name was Lorna Dickson and she stayed at the hotel during the short school "year." Because of weather, the school was open from April until September. A small gasboat, operated by one of the older pupils, Ruth Mills, picked up children from the various islands in the mornings and returned them home in the late afternoons. Now and then when a storm blew up during the day they had to stay overnight at Goddard.

It had clouded over and there was a trace of rain in the air as I walked up the hill to the big hotel. Mrs. Mary Goddard and her sister, Miss Madge Clunas, greeted me warmly and Dr. Goddard did his best to respond to my greeting. He had suffered a stroke a few months earlier and was able to speak only a few words. He was, I guess, my oldest acquaintance; he had delivered me in 1911. Dr. F.L. Goddard, a native of Massachusetts, had specialized in mental disorders and for some years had been in charge of the mental hospital at Steilacoom, Washington. He had purchased the property at the Hot Springs in the hope of establishing a similar facility there, but was unable to secure a contract from the U.S. Department of the Interior which in those years was responsible for caring for Alaska's mentally ill.

So instead of an insane asylum he built the resort hotel. There were, as I remember it, twenty-three rental rooms and six big wooden tubs for mineral baths. In summer the clients were mostly visitors from the States, while miners from Yukon Territory and northern Alaska often spent the entire winter there enjoying the hot mineral baths.

I had a hot bath and a sound sleep in a bed. After a good breakfast, including a lot of Mrs. Goddard's dollar-size hotcakes, and some visiting, including a walk with the teacher a quarter of a mile down the beach, I got started again about 10:30. The rain that had threatened the evening before had departed and the sun was again shining. I stopped for a few minutes to talk with Chris Jackson who was on his trolling boat anchored off Elevoi Island on which he had a fox farm. Then through Dorothy Narrows, named for the Goddard daughter, and on down Windy Passage and into the islands of Crawfish Inlet. As I was crossing the little basin that is formed by Lodge Island and a mess of smaller islands, a fog shut down. It came fast and thick. I had been heading for a gap between the islands but did not find it in the fog. I did find a pebbly beach with a mossy patch at its upper edge, sheltered by a big spruce tree. It was 10 o'clock by then and I was tired, so I took a blanket and my Baby Ben alarm clock and headed for the tree after dropping the anchor to hold the dory off the beach.

The moss made a good bed and I slept soundly until I was awakened be the sound of something coming toward me, shuffling the pebbles. It may or may not have been a bear but that is brown bear country and my first thought was, "bear." I wondered what time it was and picked up the clock. It was close to 1:30. I had set the alarm for 2:30, to get an early start. It occurred to me to move the minute hand forward and when the alarm began ringing there was a great scrambling of pebbles and whatever it was went tearing back up the beach. The adrenaline wasn't going to let me go back to sleep. The fog had lifted and I looked up the beach rather apprehensively. No animals were in sight. I reboarded the dory, set the gasoline stove on the thwart and cooked some oatmeal and ate it and an orange. I found the pass I had been looking for and headed on south. By 9:30 it was raining hard and a southeast wind was coming up. It had the looks of a real storm so I pulled into a sheltered cove on the north side of the entrance to Necker Bay, put up the tent and prepared to wait it out.

By noon, however, the rain had slacked off to occasional showers and the wind had died except for light gust now and then. I soon got under way. There had been enough wind to roll up a big swell, but they were no bother. At 8 p.m. I went into a cove inside North Cape and made camp. The next day, Friday, had no rain and a light breeze from the southwest. I got started at 3:30 and eleven hours later was pulling into Sandy Bay. It had been a hard pull, partly because my hands were both sore and sunburned.

On the beach inside a small island on the south shore there was a small frame cabin built, I suppose, by a trapper. There did not seem to be any other reason for a cabin in that spot. A narrow porch with a roof extended across the gable end where a door stood open. The cabin obviously had not been used for a long time and the floor of the single room was littered with tin cans, bottles and other debris. It looked, too, as though the roof leaked. The porch looked dry so I cooked some supper there, then spread out my air mattress and turned in. I woke up about 3 o'clock and had intended to get up then, but it was raining heavily. It poured into the room of the cabin but the porch remained dry. I went back to sleep and did not leave Sandy Bay until 11 in the morning.

A big swell was still rolling in and I kept some distance off the steep rocky shore. Big swells hitting that type of shore create a backlash that is uncomfortable and can be dangerous. A hair seal followed the boat for more than an hour. It would come to the surface a few feet behind the boat and stay there while I rowed on for a few hundred feet. Then it would submerge only to reappear right behind the boat again. It finally tired of the game and disappeared.

There seemed to be halibut buoy flags all over the ocean and off Snipe Bay I came up to the HI GILL of Petersburg. It was some distance outside of me, the crew was busy pulling their gear and I left them to it. As I neared Redfish Bay the seiner TATOOSH was going in. I was puzzled. She was too big for an Alaska limit salmon seiner (50 feet between perpendiculars) so was no doubt one of the herring seiners from the reduction plants on the other side of Baranof Island. But there were unlikely to be herring in Redfish Bay. The herring seiners came from down below, mostly from Puget Sound. They may have been going to do some weekend trout fishing but it is more probable that they intended to pirate some sockeye salmon to salt down and take home in the fall.

The wind was swinging around to the west and the sky was clearing. I camped on a moss-covered flat outcrop of rock, just like a dock, on Beavertail Island at the entrance to Redfish Bay. I did not bother to put up the tent. I got up at 12:30 a.m., got some breakfast and was on my way by 1:30, headed for Port Alexander.

It was a beautiful morning. The wind had died completely as westerly winds often do in the early hours of the day. There was still a long lazy swell, but the water was glassy. The sun would be coming up on the other side of mountainous Baranof Island but there were no clouds to turn pink as an indication that it was up.

When I got down close to Puffin Bay I looked ahead over my shoulder and saw a flock of birds circling low over the water. I took them for gulls and paid little attention until I looked again.

Then I saw that they were eagles. There were at least fifty of them and they were fishing, and fighting over the fish they caught. I paid attention then because they were directly in my path and I wasn't sure how much attention they would pay to me.

Both black bass and herring were flipping the surface of the water but the eagles were working on the bass. They were having fair success catching them, but success was frequently followed by a fight with another eagle for the fish. At times one or both nearly went into the water and that was what bothered me. I didn't want a couple of angry, screaming eagles crashing into my boat. I stepped the mast as some measure of protection and turned to the high thwart so I could look ahead, pushing on the oars instead of pulling on them, and moved on under the assembled National Birds. Two or three times an eagle swooped down for a fish within thirty or forty feet but none came closer than that. The successful fishers flew off toward the shore where they presumably had nests.

Soon after I got out from under the cloud of eagles the westerly wind began to blow and to kick up a short chop. That was an area famous for a nasty tide rip that extended far offshore, but I was relieved that I saw no sign of it. The westerly kept increasing and boosted me along toward Cape Ommaney, the southern tip of Baranof Island. I worried that the wind might be blowing just as hard down Chatham Strait and I would have trouble bucking it up to Port Alexander. My fears were groundless. Once I got around the cape it was flat calm and the sun was very warm -- warmer than I found comfortable. Three small halibut boats were working in Chatham Strait, their buoy flags making the glassy water look like a golf course.

A government dredge was working to widen and deepen the entrance to Port Alexander and I passed it exactly at 1:30, 12 hours after I left Beavertail Island. My hands and my muscles were getting toughened up to long hours at the oars.

There were about three hundred trolling boats at anchor, about half of them in each the outer and inner harbors. The inner harbor or lagoon, as it was called, could be entered only at half tide or better but that channel was going to be dredged, too. There were also half a dozen big herring seiners which had come to the "big town" on that side of the island for what was undoubtedly more recreation than rest over the weekend. Summertime residents of Port Alexander included quite a number of "girls," most of whom lived in shacks that were either across the harbor from the town or on floats in the lagoon. With the trollers on strike, the herring fishermen and reduction plant crews were their main customers.

There were eleven herring reduction plants on the east side of Baranof Island, in a stretch of about 50 miles, but only about half of them were running in 1931. None of the plants was at Port Alexander but the steam whistles of two of them could be heard there. When all of them were running they used about 80 big seiners that came up from Puget Sound or California for the season. This year only 35 of them came up.

The town had three docks, two big general stores, three or four restaurants, two bakeries, a pool hall, a dance hall and a schoolhouse which was closed for the summer. All except the schoolhouse were on the shore side of a boardwalk that was just above the high tide line. There was also a wireless telegraph station and the first thing I did was stop there and send a telegram to Sitka, letting my folks know where I was.

Karl Hansen had the largest store and also owned an oil dock, the wireless station, and a couple of big fish houses where he mild cured large king salmon when the trollers were fishing. The town seemed lively enough. There were lots of men on the boardwalk, quite a few of them sober, and the business places appeared busy. But everyone I talked to said it was absolutely dead compared to what it was when the fleet was fishing.

I bought a head of lettuce and some fruit at Karl Hansen's store and as I left the store I met Dr. Robert Rogers on the boardwalk. I am not sure which of us was the more surprised. He had lived in Sitka for several years and one of his two sons had been in my high school class there. He told me that he and Mrs. Rogers were in Port Alexander for the summer, sponsored by Karl Hansen and some of the herring operators. Hansen furnished them an apartment, upstairs in a store building and overlooking the harbor. Dr. Rogers had his office behind the apartment and there were also two small hospital rooms.

Dr. Rogers invited me to their apartment and we talked about Sitka and Sitka people and I had dinner with them. I left about eight o'clock, rowed up into the lagoon, found a grassy spot and pitched the tent and turned in. That was the first time I had slept in the tent and not a mosquito came in to buzz me. That was a pleasant change from my experiences sleeping in the open. But I reminded myself to buy some mosquito netting, if possible. I slept late, then wrote some letters and went into town to mail them and buy the mosquito netting. Next to the pool hall I saw a sign that said "Baths," and for fifty cents had a good soak. I turned in early with alarm set for midnight.

It was 1 o'clock Tuesday morning, June 30, by the time I got some breakfast, loaded the boat and left the lagoon. All was quiet as I turned and twisted my way through the anchored trollers and out of the harbor. There was enough twilight so I could easily see my way past the silent dredge and out into Christian Sound and the lower end of Chatham Strait. I set a course for the Kuiu Island shore.

It was a long day. I would have welcomed a breeze, especially if it proved strong enough for sailing. But there was not a breath and the water was monotonously glassy. The sun rose over the Kuiu Island mountains to the northeast and it was warm and then it was hot and there wasn't anything out there except me and my boat on that burnished sea. I was very tempted by midday to stretch out in the bottom of the boat in the shade of the tarpaulin, but instead I laid to and ate a couple of sandwiches. Behind me in the distance were the mountains of Baranof Island. Ahead in the distance were the mountains of Kuiu Island. On my port side I could look far up Chatham Strait. To starboard, in the distance, were the mountains of Coronation Island. I seemed to be about half way across that piece of water, and it was noon. There was no telling when the weather might change and I didn't want to be in the middle of Christian Sound when it did.

I pulled on the oars as hard as I could for a hundred strokes, then looked around again. Nothing had changed. The shore ahead seemed just as distant as it had been before. It was going to be a long day. I stepped up the pace because I wanted to find some kind of harbor before it got too dark.

Around 4 o'clock a white boat came in sight from around Cape Decision and I could soon make out the two masts of a halibut schooner. It was heading, by the line-up of its masts, for Cape Ommaney but after the man at the wheel saw my dory he headed in my direction. Halibut vessels carry dories and a lone dory on the ocean might be someone in distress. Nobody came on deck and when I gave no dis-

11

Salmon trollers anchored at Port Alexander.

Port Alexander, looking toward the inner harbor.

Cape Decision lighthouse under construction.

tress signals the schooner swung off again on its original course. I appreciated its concern and kept on rowing.

I reached the Kuiu Island shore just below Cape Howard and followed the shore down to Howard Cove which is full of rocks and kelp patches. It was quite dark by the time I got into the cove, five or six miles up the coast from Cape Decision. I had decided to sleep in the boat and looked for a good place to drop anchor. I was well into the cove when I discovered I was not alone. Two creatures were fighting with a lot of noise and roiling of the water. I was quite sure one was a sea lion. The other may have been another sea lion. It did not appear, from what I could see of it, large enough for an orca, a killer whale. It could have been a shark. I was dead tired and didn't want to leave the cove to hunt for another anchorage. I was close to a big kelp patch near one shore and pulled into the middle of it. I believed, perhaps incorrectly, that the battlers would not move into the kelp, but I was almost too tired to care. I didn't drop the hook but took a hitch with the painter around several stalks of bull kelp. It was 22 hours since I broke camp at Port Alexander and I was soon asleep.

It was past 8 o'clock and the weather was still fine when I got started toward Cape Decision. That was where Captain George Vancouver of the Royal Navy reached the decision, in September 1793, that Spanish explorers, despite their claims, had never traveled this far north and that the area was thus open to claim by Britain.

I was about halfway to the cape when two fellows came out from the lighthouse in a power dory to see whether I was in trouble. They were part of a ten-man crew that had been building the lighthouse and were nearly finished with the job. One of them was the radio operator and had previously served aboard the Lighthouse Tender CEDAR for two years. His name was Harry Howell and in the fall he was returning to Oregon State College at Corvallis to finish his degree. The other fellow, whose name I did not record, was a student from Corvallis, working on the construction job for the summer. I went with them into a crack in the rock below the lighthouse and made the

The dory from the lighthouse level, Cape Decision.

dory fast there. Then I got into their dory and a crane lifted it up more than a hundred feet to a platform at the lighthouse level.

Some of the crew were going to spend the Fourth of July at Ketchikan and I borrowed the use of a typewriter and wrote a short note to my folks, to be mailed at Ketchikan. I told them that my next stop would be at Shakan but that the cannery might be closed and Craig would then be the next place where I could send a message.

I had dinner with the construction crew, a big dinner and it tasted mighty good. As I was leaving the cook handed me a box which, it turned out, contained a big round loaf of pumpernickel bread, a half of each of two kinds of pie, and pieces of five or six different kinds of cake. It was 2 o'clock in the afternoon when the hoist operator lowered me down to my boat with my box.

The shortest way down the coast would have been to cross to Warren Channel and go in through Cosmos Pass and on to Tokeen, where I wanted to stop. But I wanted to see Shakan, which I had visited as a youngster, and to go through Dry Pass and El Capitan Passage, which I had never done, so I took the long way around Kosciusko Island.

As I got around Cape Decision and into Sumner Strait a moderate southwest breeze came up. I put up the sail about 2:15 for the first time and sailed up the strait until 10 p.m. when the wind died. It turned out to have been the longest stretch of sailing I had until after I left Prince Rupert. It was getting dark when I took in the sail and somehow I ran past the light at the entrance to Shakan Bay. I finally saw it behind me, turned about and went back several miles and into Shakan Strait.

It was 5:30 in the morning when I reached Shakan. I put up the tent next to a gridiron with a couple of scows on it, turned in and slept until 3 in the afternoon. The cannery was owned by Booth Fisheries Company and four tenders were on gridirons on the beach. There were a few old houses, back from the beach, but they looked to be in bad condition. Two or three Indians were living in shacks beyond the cannery, which was closed with only a watchman.

That was all that was left of what had been a village of 110 people in 1910 and perhaps had been larger in earlier years. It was not an ancient Native town but got its start around 1879 when Oliver Fontaine built a sawmill there. Natives moved there from other villages to work in the sawmill or to cut logs for the mill. It was said to have been named for a Tlinget chief, Shakes, with the addition of the suffix "an," meaning village. It was sometimes spelled Chican. Its first post office, in 1882, was called Roberts, apparently at the instigation of Dr. Sheldon Jackson who got a number of Southeastern Alaska post offices named for Presbyterian luminaries, including one for himself. The post office name was changed to Shakan in 1884 and it closed in 1936.

Now all that was left was the old and decrepit cannery. Gone were the sawmill, the salmon saltery, a general store, a hotel and the office of one of the companies that once quarried marble near by. There was scarcely a sign that they had been there, and 34 years later when I passed the site on a friend's cruiser the cannery was gone. There was scarcely a trace of it, so rapidly does the rain forest gobble up and obscure the works of man.

I talked with the watchman for a few minutes but he was surly and unsociable and I didn't stay long. I noted that fresh water was running from a pipe on the wharf, so before I cooked supper I carried my water keg to the wharf, filled it and left it on the float. I turned in after supper, got up at 2, picked up my keg and was on my way at 3:30. It began to rain soon after I started and while it never rained very hard it was rain-thick and visibility was poor. The wind had switched to the southeast. I put on oilskins and covered everything with the tarpaulins and managed to keep dry and to keep everything on board dry, but it was disagreeable rowing.

Despite all that, it was beautiful through Dry Pass and on down El Capitan Passage. I saw a former marble quarry with many blocks of white marble on the beach and a pair of decrepit buildings and some land otters on the beach. I went out through Tenas Pass, hoping to be

16

able to find Tokeen in the thick weather. "Tenas" is Chinook jargon for little or small, and the pass was both narrow and shallow. At the west end of the pass I was trying to get my bearings when the boat PROSPER of Wrangell came out through Brockman Pass and stopped near me. A man came on deck and asked where I was going.

I told him I was going to try to find Tokeen and he said that if I would give him my painter he would take me there. He was Victor "Slim" Johnson and he and his wife Minnie were going to Tokeen to celebrate the Fourth of July. She was the daughter of Fred Brockman, for whom the pass was named, and had attended Sheldon Jackson School in Sitka. We found that we had several mutual acquaintances.

Fred Brockman had been one of the old-time coopers who could cut down a big spruce tree and convert it to barrel staves with which they put together watertight barrels for salting salmon. All they needed to buy to get into the saltery business was hoop iron and salt.

We tied up at the float at Tokeen about 5 o'clock in the afternoon on Friday, July 3. It was an impressive sight as we approached the camp because the beach was lined with blocks of white marble from the three quarries that had been worked there. Most of the blocks were eight by four by four feet and they were culls, not worth shipping. The place had not operated for two years and had last worked to capacity five years earlier when marble was being quarried for the Washington State Capitol at Olympia. As many as 110 men worked there when it was in full operation but now there were only two watchmen.

The bunkhouses, office building a large main building with the kitchen, mess hall and a recreation room were unimpressive from the outside because apparently the Vermont Marble Company did not believe in painting them and they were weathered gray. Inside, however, they were very well furnished and equipped. Each workman had a room to himself and there was a pool table and a billiard table and a library of about 1200 volumes in the recreation room.

The watchmen were Harry Horn who was known, for reasons I never discovered, as "The Little Dipper," and Joe Russell, a cook and baker.

Part of Tokeen with blocks of cull marble on the beach.

One of the marble quarries, partly full of water.

A Tokeen swimming pool, at least 60 feet deep.

He made marvelous rye bread and gave me two loaves when I left the next day. He also had some skill as a brewer although at the time that activity was frowned upon by certain authorities. His product was, however, to be the main ingredient of the Fourth of July celebration at Tokeen.

Before the celebration got started, however, we had dinner and that was a real spread. There was a roast of pork, three kinds of sausage, smoked salmon, sardines, several kinds of vegetables, a big heap of sliced rye bread, watermelon and both pie and cake. The four others had beer with their meal and although there were lots of coffee mugs in sight, they preferred to drink out of heavy white soup bowls. It was a little hard to tell when the eating ended and the serious drinking began. I didn't really have a taste for beer but drank coffee and smoked my pipe.

There was a big Victrola in the recreation room not far from the end of the mess hall where we had dinner, and Harry Horn owned what seemed to be dozens of march records. He also owned a complete set of trap drums. Frequently during the evening he put on a march record, then whaled away at the drums with everything he had. As the evening wore on his timing began to slip but the volume never diminished.

There was some yarn spinning between the musical numbers, for the most part about people I did not know and events that did not seem to have much point. I do remember that someone said that a part of a skull had recently been found on an island beach, and that brought on a story about a man who had died at this camp or another one and was to be buried at Craig. First, however, there was a wake, apparently a prolonged one, and by the time the boat left for Craig a storm had blown up. The coffin was on the deck of the boat and when they got to Craig they discovered that it had been washed overboard. They went back to try to find it, and did, but it had capsized and the lid had not been fastened on and the corpse was missing. At that point the story turned into an argument. Victor Johnson claimed they never found the corpse; Harry Horn said they did find it and gave it proper burial at Craig after restoring it to its coffin.

I got tired of both the stories and the music and was told to pick any room I wanted and where to find some blankets. The bed was comfortable. I remember hearing, faintly, Harry banging away on his drums and once someone fired two or three shots from a gun, but mostly I slept very soundly.

When I woke up there was nobody in sight. I made breakfast of watermelon, rye bread, sausage and pie, then went outside to explore. The rain had stopped and the sun was coming out, but the bushes were still wet as I began looking for the quarries and found all three of them. Each was fifty or sixty feet wide and about a hundred feet long, and all were nearly full of water which came up to within six or eight feet of the rim. I was later told that one of them was a 185 feet deep. They had the appearance of big marble swimming pools but I stayed well back from the edges. There were no ladders, not even a rope, for getting out of the pool.

Tokeen to Ketchikan

We left Tokeen about noon on the Fourth of July with the PROS-PER towing the dory. It was about an hour's run to Deweyville on Sarkar Cove which indents Prince of Wales Island. Discharging into the cove through Sarkar Lagoon is Sarkar Lake which is nearly three miles long and a prime producer of red salmon. A saltery had been started there sometime in the late nineteenth century by a man named Jack Mantle who also started salteries in several other places in Southeastern Alaska.

Mantle sold the Sakhar Cove saltery to Fred Brockman, father of Minnie Johnson, sometime before 1899. He was born in Germany in December 1850 and went to sea as a ship's carpenter. He arrived in Alaska from San Francisco in 1888, perhaps to work at the Klawock cannery, one of the first two salmon canneries built in Alaska. It was no doubt he who named the place Deweyville for Commodore George Dewey, the hero of the Battle of Manila Bay. E. F. Dickins of the Coast & Geodetic Survey reported that he found the name on a sign board over the door of the fish house when he went there in 1904. Brockman continued to put up a pack of salt salmon until 1913 when he suffered a stroke. He died in 1915. In addition to Brockman Pass a small island in El Capitan Passage was named for him.

Victor Johnson and his son, who was about my age, and no doubt with the help of Minnie, salted and smoked red salmon and probably also sold some fish to a cannery when one was running in the area. Harry Swift also lived there, in a little cabin apart from the Johnsons' house, and there did not seem to be a lot of communication between them. That may have been because Swift was the stream guard for the U.S. Bureau of Fisheries and perhaps curtailed some of the Johnsons' operations. He had once been one of the owners of a cannery on Warmchuck Inlet, Hecate Island. In all probability he had gone broke, like many of the early cannerymen.

The Johnson son, whom they called Bud and whose name was no doubt Victor like his father, took me in a skiff onto Sarkar Lake. We did not go clear to the end of it, but the lake has an irregular shoreline and a confusing number of islands. I was glad I did not have to find my way off the lake. As I write this, in 1998, that entire area has been altered by a system of logging roads, one of which runs right to the site of Deweyville which is no longer a saltery but is not abandoned. There is a fishing lodge and a number of people have houses on the cove.

I had dinner with the Johnsons in their home, slept in a shed used for storing salt and barrels, and had breakfast with them the next morning. I left Deweyville at 8:30 with broken clouds in the sky, some sun and a moderate head wind in El Capitan Passage. Spanish names are all over the charts and maps of that island studded the west side of Prince of Wales Island, the result of visits by Don Juan Francisco de la Bodega y Quadra, Don Ignacio Arteaga and Francisco Antonio Maurelle between 1775 and 1779. The Spanish names are well mixed with Tlinget names, Haida names and "American" names. One wonders how much Spanish blood as well as Spanish names may have been left there.

When I got down to the upper end of Tuxekan Island I decided to go down its east side, through Tuxekan Passage, rather than to Sea Otter Sound and Karheen Passage because I wanted to see what, if anything, was left of the old village of Tuxekan. One result of that decision was that I lost about six hours. I kept over on the island side because there was less wind there and when I came to an island close to that shore I continued on inside it. I noted that the water was shoal and that my oar blades touched bottom, but the water deepened and I kept on. When I reached the lower end of the island, however, my way was blocked by a gravel bar that was just beginning to show. I turned and hurried back only to find that by then the upper end was dry, too. I was trapped until the tide came up again.

The sun was warm and the water calm in there and I got out my typewriter and put it on one thwart while I sat on another and wrote a couple of letters as I drifted. A woodpecker was hard at work in the

Remains of the Tlingit Indian village of Tuxekan.

Totem Poles at Tuxekan

timber on Tuxekan Island, a big one by the amount of noise it made. By the direction of the sound, it kept moving up the island but I never caught a glimpse of it. That was the only sound and the woodpecker may have been the only other living thing around.

I watched the tide rise ever so slowly and the moment there was enough water over the bar I was out of there. I got down to the old village of Tuxekan on the Prince of Wales Island side and took a picture of the totem poles and the remains of a few old-style houses which were nearly obscured by salmonberry bushes. This had been the chief village of the Henya (sometimes Henega) Tlingits with as many as 300 people living there in the winter.

In November 1886 Dr. Sheldon Jackson sent the Rev. L.W. Currie to Tuxekan to start a school. No white man had ever lived in the village and there were no frame houses. He and his family had to be content with an Indian house that measured 80 by 37 feet and had walls of hewn planks and a rotten bark roof. They moved to Klawock the following year and he built a school house and a dwelling there and Tuxekan never did get a school. It didn't get any industry, either; no sawmill, no cannery, and the people had gradually moved away, to Shakan and Klawock and elsewhere, leaving the totem poles to the ravages of the climate. "We did not abandon Tuxekan," Charles Demmert, a former resident, said in 1944. "We simply moved away. We had our last big potlatch there in 1902."

I did not go ashore at Tuxekan, which is right at Tuxekan Narrows at the north end of Tuxekan passage. I expected a strong current in the narrows but detected none and pulled on southward. At 5:30 I made camp on a small island, provoked at myself for the six hours of lost time. I somewhat made up for that by getting started at 3:30 the next morning. I had intended to stop at the Karheen cannery on the west side of Tuxekan Island, a couple of miles above its southern tip. A family friend, Guy Chapin, had been superintendent of the cannery before it was sold to Libby, McNeill and Libby in 1929 and I thought he might still be there.

After I passed the lower end of Tuxekan Island I could look up Karheen Passage and see the cannery, but I was anxious to get to Craig and so kept going toward Tonowek Narrows, locally known as Little Skookumchuck. The real Skookumchuck, Tlevak Narrows, was farther south. Skookum was the Chinook jargon word for strong or powerful, and Chuck was water. Hence, strong water, a swift current.

It must have been slack water when I went through the Skookumchuck and I did not detect any current. I kept over along the Prince of Wales Island shore and inside all the islands and rocks. There was quite a lot of boat traffic outside me, mostly seiners and cannery tenders. I passed several floating fish traps and went close to one of them but the watchman did not come out of his shack and I didn't hail him.

I had a couple of hours of good sailing going down San Cristoval Channel and across San Alberto Bay and reached Fish Egg Island, across a narrow channel from the town of Craig, about 7 p.m. I looked for a camping place on the island but found none and finally anchored and slept in the boat. I looked again in the morning but still found nothing suitable. I washed up and rowed across to the town and tied up at a float.

Things were quiet in Craig. The trollers were still on strike but some of the fishermen were having a meeting in the street while I was there and trolling boats began going out in the late afternoon. The cannery, owned by Libby, McNeill and Libby, was operating but was getting very little fish. I sent a telegram to Mother and also wrote a letter and sent it to Ketchikan with a Mr. Howard on a Pioneer Airways plane. Several planes were in and out during the day. I talked to Z. M. Bradford, the Standard Oil agent, as we had some mutual friends in Juneau where he had previously been stationed. He introduced me to Dr. de Wyndum and to Judge Bagley, the U.S. Commissioner who had had correspondence with my dad, the Commissioner at Sitka. I was glad later on that I had met him because without knowing it he was of help to me.

Town of Craig, cannery at right.

Cannery tenders maneuver a floating trap into place.

The village of Craig started life with the name Fish Egg. The island was named in 1897, probably because herring spawned in the area each spring. There were Native fish camps on the island and perhaps on the site of the present town. In 1907 Craig Millar, a member of the numerous Millar family of which more later, built a saltery on the island. This was moved to the town site the following year and some permanent homes were built there. The name Fish Egg was retained. Millar became associated with the Lindenberger brothers, processors and marketers of mild cured salmon. He built a cold storage plant and then a cannery for them. In 1912 the company packed 4,280 tierces of mild cured salmon (it takes approximately a thousand pounds of raw fish to fill a tierce) and 57,501 cases of canned salmon. That was the year the town got a U.S. Commissioner and a post office which abandoned the old name and adopted a new one, Craig.

A sawmill was very active during World War I, cutting spruce lumber to be used in building airplanes. The town has had its ups and downs over the years. It was listed as having 231 residents at the time of my visit but reached a peak of 505 by the end of that decade. It had dwindled to 272 by 1970 but then staged a comeback and by 1996 had an estimated 2,109 residents.

I emptied my water keg as the water tended to get a little stale after a warm day or two and refilled it at the Standard Oil dock and also replenished the supply of gasoline for the stove. I bought a few supplies and got into a conversation with a young woman clerk in Cogo's store, which was not at all busy. She was a good-looking woman of mixed blood, with probably some Haida in the mix. She was very curious about my boat and where I was going and wanted to know whether I had a tent. I explained it all but didn't realize where it was leading until she announced that she wanted to go with me. That took the wind out of my sails for a few moments.

I recovered enough, after a bit, to tell her that neither her family nor mine would look kindly on our taking off together. She had an answer for that. She said we could go to Judge Bagley and get married, and if I didn't want to stay married after we got to Tacoma she would get a divorce. That gave me an out. I explained that Judge Bagley was a friend of my family and knew that I was only nineteen and that he could not issue a marriage license to any man under 21. I expressed extreme regret and got out of there.

I was a little apprehensive when I left the store and for the rest of the time I was in Craig. Was she a woman scorned, and what might be the consequences? How determined was she? Later on when I was stormbound at Cape Chacon I began to think it would be nice to have a companion, but I wasn't about to row all the way back to Craig to get one.

The town is on a little peninsula and there was a small cove on the north side of it. I pulled around to that back side of the town and found a float that had a sign on it that said it belonged to the Forest Service. Nobody was around and I unloaded most of my gear onto the float, then re-stowed and rearranged it. If I was going to continue to sleep in the boat I wanted a little more room to stretch my six-foot body. I also rearranged the tarpaulins to give better cover when it rained. It was peaceful at the float and I could have stayed there until morning, but I had visions of my would-be passenger coming aboard, bag and baggage, in the middle of the night.

So I left the float, pulled off a little way, dropped anchor and turned in. I slept well and until after 8 o'clock on Wednesday, July 8. Got started about 10 with a headwind, rain squalls and hard pulling. As I passed a floating fish trap the watchman, a young Native, came out and we talked for awhile. He said that his name was Fred and that his father was William L. Paul. That surprised me but I didn't say so. William Paul had been in the Territorial Legislature a couple of terms, although not in 1931 when I was in Juneau.

He had campaigned vigorously for the abolishment of fish traps and I wondered whether the owners of this trap might have feared that his son would cut it loose.

After nine hours I had made only 10 miles and I anchored inside

Cape Flores for the night. I didn't start until 9 the next morning because where I was anchored the wind seemed to be blowing even harder. When I got around Cape Flores, however, it was nearly calm. I got down to the Nakat Packing Company cannery at Waterfall at 10:15. This was a big cannery with three lines of tall cans and one of flats. Everything was painted and immaculate. I went through the cannery which had several pieces of more modern machinery than I was familiar with at the Pyramid cannery at Sitka. I talked with a mechanic about them. Nobody else spoke to me. In fact, there were very few people in sight because they were waiting for the first fish of the season to start work. The crew was Chinese. Nakat, which has several canneries in Alaska, all the way out to Bristol Bay, was a branch of the A&P chain of grocery stores and I believe they sold the pack only in their own stores. That was certainly an incentive to put up as palatable a can of salmon as possible. A fine big tender came in with the season's first load of fish just as I was pulling out and the cannery's steam whistle was blowing to call the crew to work.

The Skookumchuck was next. It was supposed to be time for slack water but I had to buck some current. The narrows is not very long and the shores are steep and rocky. There were white crosses on both shores, testifying to the perils of the place. There was a gravestone at one place with a signboard. It said that a man and the seine and seine skiff had washed overboard and the man had never been found. At the western end of the Chuck I met the mailboat FAIRBANKS from Ketchikan and the U.S Bureau of Fisheries boat PETREL.

The area I had been traveling through since leaving Sitka was the aboriginal home of the Tlingit Indians. Now I was getting into Haida country, although it had once been inhabited by the Tlingits. The Haidas were from the Queen Charlotte Islands in Canada and some of them had moved to southern Southeast Alaska, apparently around 1700, and had forced the Tlingit residents to move northward. This fact was attested by the Tlingit names on the Haida villages of Kasaan, Klinkwan, Howkan and Sukkwan.

Once through the chuck I had light but fair wind down past Halibut Nose and did some sailing. The wind had died by the time I got to Turn Rock and an Indian came up behind me in a small numbered troller and asked if I wanted a tow into Hydaburg. It was 5 o'clock by then and still several miles to Hydaburg and I welcomed the offer.

I got aboard and he started off. He said that the coffee pot was on the stove and suggested that I get myself a cup. It was on the stove and it must have been boiling there for a week. I had never tasted anything as bitter, although I did meet its equal later at Very Inlet. There was no cream in sight and I poured the stuff back into the pot.

"Strong coffee," I said when I went topside. He just grinned. We got to Hydaburg at 6:15. The floating cannery PIONEER which was on a small ship's hull was tied to the wharf. It was not operating and was in charge of a watchman, Ted Samuelson, a large man with a small head. He was not very talkative but had nothing good to say about the Indians who lived in Hydaburg and said that he never went ashore there. In later years I became acquainted with his son, Ken, who was a deputy U.S. Marshal at Ketchikan and Sitka.

Hydaburg is not an ancient town and was built for the purpose of education. The two principal Haida towns were Howkan and Klinkquan but there were also a few people at Sukkwan and perhaps at the old village of Koianglas. The Bureau of Indian Affairs felt that it could not maintain more than one school in the area and in 1911 persuaded a majority of the people to move and consolidate in one town. The present site was picked, on Prince of Wales Island and at the upper end of Sukkwan Strait. The post office of Hydaburg was opened on May 16, 1912, with Charles W. Hawkesworth, the schoolteacher, as postmaster. A few years after my visit a cannery was built on shore but was destroyed by fire in 1948. It was rebuilt but, like many salmon canneries, has had only moderate success. The estimated population of the town in 1996 was 410.

Samuelson invited me to eat supper with him and suggested that I take one of the staterooms. He also provided a big breakfast the next morning, livened by his tales about what a bad place Cape Chacon was for a boat of any size. I was tempted to go ashore and explore but I had to get around Cape Chacon, the south point of Prince of Wales Island, so I shoved off. It was a day of mostly headwinds and tide and I made only 11 miles. I passed a big rock that must have been a rookery for hair seals as there were dozens of them around it. Two of them followed me until I anchored for the night in Mud Bay. I had tried to get around Lime Point but the wind was too strong. It rained in the night but I kept dry and slept comfortably in the boat. The wind was still blowing from the south in the morning but I pulled down to Lime Point again and tried to get around it. The wind was coming in hard gusts with no real lull between them and the gusts blew the boat backward.

I spotted a cabin up in the woods on the north side of the point and it looked inviting. There was, however, no landing place or harbor near it. I pulled back toward Mud Bay and found a little cove with a sandy beach and a good camping place. I set up the tent and filled the stove tank from the can I had had refilled in Craig. The stove wouldn't light and I discovered, after some fussing around, that Bradford had given me kerosene instead of gasoline. So I had no way to cook, and even worse than that, I was out of things to read. I had neglected to pick up any magazines in Craig, so I went to sleep.

The next day was no better for weather, with the wind perhaps even stronger. I didn't try to travel but went up into the woods to look for berries. They were scarce. Back in the tent, for want of something else to do I fooled with the stove. I found that by pumping it up far more than normal, I could get the kerosene to burn. It didn't get very hot but in time would boil water and I could make coffee. I wrote some letters and slept some more.

This lower part of the West Coast of Prince of Wales Island had in earlier years been the home of the very active Millar family.

James Millar and at least one of his three sons, Andrew, who was then 14, came north to Burroughs Bay on Behm Canal in 1883. The family had lived for many years at Peterboro, Ontario, Canada, and most, if not all, of the boys and two girls were born there. They had recently moved to Victoria, B.C., and Millar and Andrew came north in 1883 to establish a salmon saltery. They probably spent the winters at Victoria. The second son, Bert, was at Burroughs Bay in 1884 and the youngest son, Craig, was probably also there before they abandoned that location after 1887.

There is some indication that the family moved from Victoria to Wrangell for a few years, but for the most part they lived at the Haida village of Klinkquan (the spelling later changed to Klinkwan) on the lower West Coast of Prince of Wales Island. James Millar opened a store there and upstairs over the store there was a schoolroom whenever a teacher was available. He and his sons operated salteries at several places on the lower West Coast, including Hunters Bay, Nichols Bay, Hetta Inlet and Klakas Inlet.

Craig Millar was postmaster at Klukwan for a couple of years and the town of Craig, as previously mentioned, was named for him. Bert Millar Cutoff, Millar Rocks and possibly Minnie Bay were named for members of the family. The best known, in recent times, was Margaret Bell, the daughter of Florence Millar Bell and author of many works of fiction with settings in Alaska.

By Monday morning, July 13, the weather had moderated and I broke camp and got started not long after daylight. I got past Lime Point and as I started across the mouth of Nutkwa Inlet I could hear what sounded like two or three big diesel engines but I couldn't see the boats at first. Then I spotted them down near Mable Island. They were not traveling but stayed in one place and when I got closer I saw that there were two cannery tenders and a rigging scow and they were setting a floating trap. I pulled just close enough to watch but not get in the way as they put out the big anchors, then stretched the lead to a tailhold on the beach.

I knew how a floating trap caught fish as I had once been a watchman's helper on one, but I had never seen one being put in place. It was a pleasure to watch those two boats work together. The trap was nearly a hundred feet square and built of big logs and the boats held it in place while the rigging scow set the five-ton anchors and I watched for the best part of an hour.

I passed another trap near Point Webster but nobody was in sight. Later in the afternoon I came up to another trap and two young fellows were getting seaweed and other flotsam out of the trap and I stopped to talk with them. They said that during the storm some of the waves had washed over the trap logs, throwing the debris into the trap. It belonged to the cannery at Rose Inlet and had just started fishing and had not yet been brailed, but there were only a few salmon in it.

I was invited to have supper there and I tied the dory behind the trap shack and went aboard. Supper was mostly out of cans but there was plenty of it and it beat my own cooking. After supper they asked if I needed any grub and hauled out cans of vegetables, fruit and meat and insisted that I take them. "We'll just order more from the cannery when the tender comes, probably tomorrow morning." It was 9 o'clock when I thanked them and pulled away. Half an hour later I pulled into a little cove behind the island at Shipwreck Point and turned in.

Tuesday, July 14, was bright and clear although a fog bank hung offshore all day. I got started at 5:30 and by 8:30 was going through the many small islands and rock piles inside the Barrier Islands. A towboat with five sections of logs passed outside of me and I surmised that she was going to Prince Rupert because she stayed so far out after passing Marsh Point. The day was uneventful, just pulling or pushing on the oars, and I anchored inside Marsh Point about 4 o'clock. I hoped to get around Cape Chacon the next morning and wanted another day of good weather. After Ted Samuelson's stories and seeing the legendary tide rips around the cape on the chart of that area, I was a little apprehensive and got started at 4 o'clock.

My apprehensions proved groundless. The weather was bright and sunny with a light westerly breeze. And I made great progress, all the way to Ketchikan, but most of it under tow. In the morning I went through the Bert Millar Cutoff, inside Bean Island. I could see tide rips outside me but was not bothered by them. There was a fairly strong current but it was going my way and I was past the terrible Cape Chacon almost before I knew it.

Despite Cape Chacon's reputation as a danger to shipping, I have found only one report of a bad shipwreck there, and that was very early in Alaska's years under the American flag. The battered wreck of the 50-ton American schooner GROWLER was discovered on the cape in March 1868. No survivors were found but it was believed that some of the 12 men and one woman on board had escaped from the wreck only to be killed by Indians who then proceeded to loot the cargo.

The GROWLER had been bound for Sitka with a cargo of general merchandise, including some kegs of liquor. In command of Captain Horace Coffin, who was commonly known as Tom, she had made one previous trip to Sitka and had carried a cargo from there to San Francisco in January. Just who among the white population discovered the wreck and reported it to Sitka is not known, but the people of Sitka collected about $150 and sent Charles Trueworthy to Cape Chacon to ascertain what he could about the wreck and to bring any bodies he found to Sitka for burial.

When Trueworthy returned to Sitka he had a few silver coins and a knife identified as belonging to Captain Coffin. He had buried such remains as he found and marked the place with headboards, and he did not believe that anyone reached shore alive. That was reportedly borne out by a story attributed to an Indian woman but she added that the survivors who struggled to get ashore were met with gunfire by Indians.

The wreck was also investigated by Commander John G. Mitchell, USN, commanding the USS SAGINAW. He picked up a couple of anchors with chains at the site of the wreck and another one at a nearby Indian village. Then he crossed Dixon Entrance to Canadian waters and the Haida village of Massett on the Queen Charlotte Islands. There he found a quadrant, part of a clock and other items belonging to the GROWLER. He took aboard two Massett Indians, identified in the ship's log as "passengers" but actually prisoners and potential witnesses. One can imagine what an international fuss there would be if any such action were taken today.

The two men from Massett and two from Cape Chacon were taken to Sitka and held there for a time, but there was then no court in Alaska and, so far as is known, there was no hearing of any kind regarding the loss of the GROWLER. The witnesses were returned to their homes and the full circumstances of the GROWLER wreck remain unknown.

As I moved from the cape up along the eastern side of Prince of Wales Island I could see a piling trap ahead of me with a tender alongside it. Piling traps were becoming a rarity. In the earlier years of the fishery all of the traps had been formed of piling driven into the bottom in the shape of a corral. Webbing was fastened to them to entrap the salmon. After J.R. Heckman invented the floating trap in 1907 they had gradually replaced most of the piling traps.

The tender proved to be the LLOYD C. of the Sunny Point Packing Company at Ketchikan. I could see two men in a skiff working along the lead and there was a man enjoying the sun on deck. I pulled up alongside and he said they were waiting until the tide turned to make the first lift of the season at this trap and that the boss and the skipper of the LLOYD C. were inspecting the lead. I asked who the boss was and was told it was Sam Bartholomew, the superintendent of the Sunny Point cannery.

That gave me an opening and I said I wanted to meet Bartholomew and climbed aboard. Earlier that year at Juneau the messenger on the staff of the House of Representatives was an elderly gentleman from Ketchikan named A. Bartholomew. I became quite well acquainted with him, mostly because he wanted something: a story in the paper. He had been, he told me, a star on his high school football team and would like the fact written up. I wrote a story, making him the hero of a game, and fortunately I showed it to him before turning it in. It was all wrong because what he had played was what he called association football. I knew nothing about that game, but with his coaching I wrote another story which satisfied him. Mrs. White, the owner and editor, looked a little puzzled when I turned in the story, like, "What is that all about?" but she let it pass and Mr. Bartholomew was very pleased. Somewhere along the way he mentioned that he had a son who was a cannery superintendent.

So I was able to introduce myself to Sam Bartholomew as a friend of his father. He immediately invited me to stay aboard for lunch. Before we had that they brailed the trap. The method was somewhat different than what I had been used to with the floating traps operated by the Pyramid Packing Company. There they used a round dipnet with a purse line at the bottom. Here they used a flat brail. They got about 1,200 fish in that first lift of the season.

After lunch Bartholomew said they were going up to McLean Arm to another trap, then into Ketchikan, and he asked whether I wanted a tow. I was happy to accept. It is a long haul across that lower end of Clarence Strait, and the weather looked very uncertain. I had planned to follow the Prince of Wales Island shore up to Rip Point at the entrance to Moira Sound. From there it was only about a dozen miles across the strait to Annette Island, but with a beam wind and sea if the weather was bad it could be a rough crossing.

We had dinner on the way to Ketchikan and, like lunch, it was bountiful. The crew of the LLOYD C. included a cook and for dinner he gave us a choice of pork chops or roast beef, or both if you wanted, mashed potatoes and gravy, a salad of beets and lettuce, a couple of vegetables and both pie and cake.

I left the LLOYD C. at the cannery, across Tongass Narrows from the present airport, about 6:30 o'clock. I had friends in Ketchikan but it seemed a little late to look them up so I pulled across the channel to the Gravina Island shore and found an anchorage for the night.

Brailing the salmon from a standing fish trap.

Ketchikan to Prince Rupert

I turned out at 5:30 on Thursday, July 16, just as a light rain was starting, but it stopped after a few showers and the sky cleared. I pulled across the channel and berthed at the float where the city fire boat was moored. A big sign said, "No boats or persons allowed on this float except on business." There was a man aboard the fire boat and he gave permission to stay during the day. He said it was unlikely that anyone would bother the dory there and that he would keep an eye on it. I first went to the post office for my mail which included one from Mother postmarked the 14th, so it made good time. A letter from the University of Oregon confirmed my admission in September and enclosed some forms to be filled out. I then looked up J.P. McNeil, who was buying fish for the Booth Fisheries Company. He had been manager of Booth's cold storage at Sitka until it was sold the first of the year to Sitka people. I got a haircut and a bath, then climbed the hill to the court house to see William Caswell who had been the deputy U.S. Marshal in Sitka for several years and had the same position here. He went with me to the bank and I cashed a check, getting most of the money in Canadian currency. The next stop was at the custom house to get clearance for Prince Rupert.

From there I went to the office of the Ketchikan Chronicle and found Sidney Charles and his son Paul, known as Bud. The Charles family had come to Sitka in May 1922, and Sidney had started the Sitka Tribune, a weekly paper. Bud "worked the case," as printers say, hand setting type for his father. Bud and I had been in the fifth grade together during the next school year, after which Sidney sold the paper and they moved to Petersburg.

It turned out that I would work for Sidney and Bud many years later when they were publishing The Alaska Fishing News and then the Ketchikan Daily News. I was invited to dinner at the Charles home that evening.

In the afternoon I wrote some letters and bought some stores and put them aboard the boat. I rowed down to the Sunde & d'Evers ma-

A standing or piling fish trap south of Ketchikan.

My camp on the beach at Very Inlet.

The cabin at Very Inlet and my host, Bill Folks.

rine outfitting store to buy a pair of oars. I had left Sitka with two pair of spruce oars, one pair eight feet long, the other seven. The eight-footers were my favorites but I had failed to secure one of them properly when towing across Clarence Strait and it had rolled overboard. I didn't find any long spruce oars and finally settled for a pair of nine-foot dory oars. They were of ash and much heavier and stiffer than the spruce oars. Then I went to the Standard Oil dock, dumped the coal oil and had my can filled with gasoline and also took on water.

I had dinner with Mr. and Mrs. Charles, Bud and Marjorie, the only one of the three Charles daughters still living at home. After dinner I went for a drive with Bud and some of his friends and later for another drive with Sidney and Mrs. Charles. He told stories about his newspaper experiences clear across the country from his birthplace in Minnesota and in half a dozen towns in Alaska. At the end of the evening I pulled over to a cove at the north end of Pennock Island and turned in at 11:30.

Next morning, the 17th, I was ready to head on south but had not tried out the new oars. They were too thick through the shaft to fit my rowlocks, so I went back to the store and bought larger rowlocks, as well as a pair of leathers to protect the oars from wear at the rowlocks.

Heading south again along the Ketchikan waterfront I had an adventure that probably was highly dangerous. At any rate, it scared me. The steamer NORTHWESTERN was pulling out from the dock ahead of me and I laid to wait until she was gone. But instead of moving on the ship stopped with her bow pointing straight out into the channel and her stern probably fifty or sixty feet from the wharf. And she sat there. It may not have been more than five minutes but it seemed forever and I decided that if the ship was not going to move, I was.

When I was directly astern of the ship and perhaps ten feet away from the dock they turned on the power. That big propeller threw a terrific wash and it slammed the dory against the camels, floating logs that protected the piling, almost before I knew what was happening. I knew from reading rather than from experience that in those circumstances a small boat was apt to be rolled under the log. I got an oar straight down into the current and braced against the gunwale to keep the dory upright or as nearly upright as possible. I held that oar in place with both hands for what seemed ages until the ship had moved far enough that the propeller wash was no longer a problem.

Standing on the wharf watching all this and ready to yell for help if I tipped over was Peter F. Gilmore. He was my age but I did not know him then. Many years later we became close friends and compared notes on the incident when we were both living in Juneau.

I eventually got my nerves settled down and headed south. When I left Sitka I had thought that from Ketchikan I might make a side trip through Behm Canal, around Revillagigedo Island. I now gave up that notion. I was 25 days out of Sitka and calculated that I had traveled 350 miles to Cape Chacon. That was an average of 14 miles a day. It is roughly 750 miles from Ketchikan to Seattle by the steamer channels. That meant I would have to average nearly 16 miles a day to reach Tacoma by Labor Day, my original plan.

I pulled past the wharves and the sawmill, which was in full operation, to where a dredge was at work on the Thomas Basin project. They were also building a breakwater to make a harbor for small boats there at the mouth of Ketchikan Creek. The basin would be where, in earlier years, they played baseball at low tide. Games may never have been called because of rain but they sometimes were because of tide.

As I was passing the village of Saxman, south of Ketchikan, a Native fellow came out in a rowboat and asked to take my picture. He said he had lived in Sitka. I asked him to send a print of his picture to my mother. He promised to do so and kept his promise. I crossed the channel and anchored at the south end of Pennock Island for the night.

I got a late start on Saturday, the 18th, and made only 11 miles against a headwind. I anchored for the night inside Cone Island. On Sunday I turned out at 4:15 and was on my way an hour later. Many fish traps were along this shore and I stopped at one where a tender was brailing. There are also many fine sandy beaches and I pulled in and stopped at a couple of them. I crossed the entrance to Boca de Quadra and pulled into Kah Shakes Cove, a short distance to the south. There were some Indian summer houses ashore but nobody was in sight and I did not stop.

I was right in the steamer channel now and ships were passing all the time. I saw the ADMIRAL ROGERS, which got to Sitka every two weeks, three times in one day. Early in the morning she passed me going toward Ketchikan. Then just before I got to Boca de Quadra she came back and went in where there was a cannery. I was just going into Kah Shakes when she came out of Boca de Quadra and headed north again. I suppose she had to enter customs at Ketchikan before stopping at the cannery.

Monday morning there was a strong wind from the south when I got up at 5 but later it moderated and I pulled out of the cove at 8:45. It was still a headwind and hard pulling. At 1:30 I got in the lee of one of the DeLong Islands that was entirely sand. I went ashore and sat on the sand on the highest part of the island. Gulls were circling high and that is often an indication of an approaching storm. So I got back aboard and pulled a mile or so to Very Inlet. I anchored near the north shore a little distance inside the entrance at 3:30, read and watched the weather. Turned in at 7:30 but by 8:30 I could tell that the wind had increased considerably and was gusty and flawing. So I turned out again, went ashore and put up the tent. I staked it down well, moved most of the gear into it and prepared to wait out the weather. I had bought an American Mercury and some other magazines in Ketchikan so did have something to read. It was a good enough camping place, with a little stream of clear water about a hundred feet from the tent.

On Tuesday it rained hard all day and I mostly stayed in the tent, read, cooked and slept. The rain let up a little bit but the wind did not. I picked some berries and when I was on my way back to the tent a porcupine came waddling down the beach. I got the camera and took one picture of it, then watched it awhile as it moved slowly along.

Porcupines don't grow on Baranof and Chichagof Islands and I knew little about them. This one finally climbed a tree and I went back into the tent. Once when I looked out a big buck was coming down the beach. I grabbed the camera but he had gone into the woods before I could get a picture. The wind died in the evening and there was some blue sky.

The change in the weather proved false. Wednesday was about the same as Tuesday. On Thursday, July 23, it was blowing hard again, and raining. I was exactly a month out of Sitka and was stalled, a long way from Tacoma. Another day in camp. The wind began to pick up around noon so I cut down a small cedar tree and split it up into long stakes then drove four of them well into the ground, two on each side of the tent. Then I put a couple of lines across the top of the ridgepole and made them fast to the stakes.

I was eating dinner about 5 o'clock when I heard a boat going past and when I looked out it was a gray-painted Bureau of Fisheries boat and it was going out of the inlet. I must have been asleep when it went past going in. I had about finished eating when I heard a gasboat coming down the inlet. The skipper anchored a short distance below my camp, came ashore in a punt and walked up toward the tent. I went out to meet him. He looked like an old-timer, with slouch clothes, an old sou'wester and a long gray beard. He looked to be in his late sixties, at least.

"Are you going somewhere or just traveling?" he asked when he got close. I said I wasn't doing either so long as this wind kept up.

"The warden said you were down here and told me to take a look at you," he said apologetically. "I don't know why, because you sure haven't got any fishing gear, but them federal fellows is awfully nosy."

He introduced himself as Bill Folks and said he was the stream guard. He said he had a big log cabin a quarter of a mile up the inlet and suggested that I break camp and move in with him until the weather broke. "It might be another couple of days." I was comfortable enough where I was, but sitting in the tent was getting monotonous and a move would be a change. Bill helped me strike the tent and pack things to the boat and I hitched on behind his little numbered gasboat and we were soon at his cabin. It was a big cabin of unpeeled spruce logs and a shake roof. One big room with a kitchen range, a couple of bunks built against the wall and a big cluttered table against the window.

We had no more than gotten into the cabin when Bill offered me a cup of coffee, but I got a glimpse of the contents of his coffee pot when he took the lid off and I told him that drinking coffee was against my religion. The "pot" was a big granite ware kettle that was around 15 inches in diameter and designed to hold 12 quarts or so. Packed solidly around the wall of the kettle were coffee grounds, leaving a pothole perhaps eight inches in diameter for the coffee or whatever it was filled with. It was so close to jet black as to make no difference and he dipped out a mug full and drank it with relish. He drank two or three more before we turned in.

I watched carefully in the morning after he got the wood fire started. He poured water into the pothole in the coffee grounds and threw in a handful of fresh grounds. Later on I asked whether he ever cleaned out the kettle. "Once in awhile, when it gets down to not more than about four cups of liquid. But it's a job because I dig out the oldest grounds from around the edge and move the rest of them back. I don't do it oftener than I have to." The rest of his cooking turned out better than his coffee. We had fried eggs and bacon and hotcakes and he kept insisting that I had room enough for two or three more hotcakes.

Bill Folks, who came from Wyoming and Montana, had been in Alaska since the turn of the century and had done just about everything a man could do to make a living: fished, hand logged, prospected and mined, operated tenders for one cannery and fired the boiler at another one. Now he worked for the federal government as a stream guard in the summer and did a little trapping in the winter. This cabin, he told me, belonged to "Nigger" Watson who was not a Negro and who used it as headquarters for running his trap lines in the winter. Folks had his own trapping cabin on Behm Canal and another cabin on Pennock Island at Ketchikan, where he spent most of his time.

It continued to rain and blow on Friday and much of Saturday. We went up into Very Inlet in Bill's gasboat on Friday. It is a maze of chucks, streams and canals for miles back from the entrance and there were a few beaver houses in one place. We saw only one beaver and not very much of it. One narrow channel has sheer walls of black rock and very strong currents. We went in on the last of the flood, didn't stay very long and went out with the first of the ebb.

Bill made a big stew with venison he had canned himself and potatoes and onions. I contributed cans of sweet potatoes, carrots and peas that had come from fish traps along the way, and we ate on that for two days. On Saturday afternoon the wind shifted to the west and the sky began to clear and Sunday morning I got started again toward the south. But not until late. Bill insisted that I have a big breakfast and then that he tow me out of the inlet and so it was 11 o'clock when I cut loose and waved good-bye to him.

There was a floating trap about every mile along that shore and each one I passed the watchman would run out and shout that he had just put on the coffee pot. I shucked my recently found religion and had several mug-ups but didn't make a lot of mileage. I had supper with two young fellows who were the watchmen on the Gamble trap of the Nakat Packing Company. After supper we went down to the Tree Point Lighthouse, only a few hundred yards from the trap. The keeper showed us all through the lighthouse, the last one before getting into Canada. I stayed the night at the trap.

On Monday, July 27, I left the Gamble trap at 10 and about 1 o'clock stopped at a mooring scow that was anchored behind Cape Fox and had lunch there. In the afternoon I went on down to Tongass Island to the deserted Indian village which is fronted by a fine sandy beach. There were a dozen or more totem poles, some of them lying on the ground and all of them badly deteriorated.

The Lincoln totem, which is now at the State Museum in Juneau, was still standing but leaning and probably about ready to topple over.

The story of that pole is that a resident of the village claimed to have been the first one to see a white man and wanted a pole carved to commemorate that fact. He hired a carver but the carver needed a picture of a white man and applied to the Army post, on the other side of the island. The only picture the soldiers could produce was one of President Lincoln, so the figure on top of the pole was carved in his image, top hat and all. I had heard about the Seward "shame pole" but it was not standing and if it was on the ground it was hidden by tall grass and berry bushes. The story was that when William H. Seward, the former Secretary of State, visited Tongass Village in 1869 he had been presented with many gifts but was unaware that he was expected to reciprocate. To commemorate the fact that Seward gave no gifts, the residents had a pole carved. At its top was a chest such as the Indians used for storing their furs and blankets. And sitting on the lid of the chest, so it could not be opened, was the figure of a man, representing Seward.

The residents of Tongass Village and of Cape Fox Village all moved to a new village, Saxman, near Ketchikan about the turn of the century. Soon after the Alaska purchase an Army post and a customs office had been established on Tongass Island but at a different site than the Native village. I wasn't sure just where they had been and did not go looking for them because I didn't expect that many traces of them were left. The Army post, Fort Tongass, had been abandoned in the summer of 1870 and a few years later the Custom House was moved to Mary Island and still later to Ketchikan. Charles Walden had operated a trading post there until he was a victim of the wreck of the GEORGE S. WRIGHT. He was followed by James Turk who also had a salmon saltery but he eventually moved away. There may have been people living in the abandoned buildings of the fort until a Revenue Cutter was ordered, in the 1880s, to go there and burn them.

From Tongass Island I headed down Lincoln Channel, a narrow passage between Kanagunut Island on the west and Sitklan Island on the east. About halfway down the passage, on the Sitklan Island side there was a float with a gasboat tied to it, and on shore behind the float was a house and another building that could have been a wood-shed. A small barefooted man came out of the house and down the gangway to the float. His eyes lighted up when he saw the dory and he asked where I got it. I told him I had it built at Sitka. "I could tell it isn't a standard dory," he said. "They are mostly lap-straked. But it's the right shape." He went on to say that he had been a dory fisherman in the halibut steamer NEW ENGLAND. He didn't say what he was doing on Sitklan Island and didn't tell me his name, so I didn't ask. I didn't see any barrels for salting fish or any commercial fishing gear, and later when he invited me into the house for supper, I saw no traps or stretching boards. The boat at the float was built for speed and I concluded that he was making a living by smuggling, probably mostly rum running. The Canadian boundary was only a few miles away.

Soon after supper I excused myself, went to the boat and turned in, still tied to the float. That was a mistake. There wasn't any wind but there was a current that now and then bumped the boat against the float. I wasn't used to that and it kept waking me up. I was too sleepy, or too lazy, however, to get up and anchor the boat and eliminate the annoyance.

Staying at the float was a mistake in another way, too. I wanted to get an early start because I had some open water to cross. The sky was clear and there was a good probability that there would be some westerly wind by afternoon. I had the air mattress deflated and stowed and the blankets rolled up and in their duffel bag and was considering what to grab for a quick breakfast when the thin man came down and suggested I eat with him. I accepted, partly because I was hungry and partly because I thought he might be more talkative than he had been the night before and I might learn something about him.

The breakfast was good but he was awfully slow preparing it, and he was talkative; far too talkative. Before, during and after breakfast he strung together yarns about his years as a dory fisherman in a way that made it hard to break in and get away without being rude. And I wasn't rude.

In consequence, the morning was well gone by the time I got out of Lincoln Channel and into open water, the eastern edge of Dixon Entrance. The storm of the past few days had rolled up a big ocean swell which in itself was no bother to me. But a westerly wind was beginning to rise and that was pushing up the swells and by the time I had gone a few miles some of them were showing signs of combing. It was fun riding on the front of those big swells, but it could also be dangerous if the boat got out of control.

I turned to face the bow which got lower and lower while the stern rose higher and higher as the swell pushed us along. The boat had some tendency to sheer as the bow got lower and I had my hands full steering with the oars. When the bow had dipped down until there was only six or eight inches of freeboard, I pulled hard on the oars and backed off of that swell and waited for the next one. It is nearly a dozen miles from Lincoln Channel to Bernie Island where I sought shelter, and for nearly four hours I didn't dare take my hands off the oars. Sometime during those four hours I had crossed from Alaska to British Columbia, Canada.

It was nearly 3 o'clock when I pulled into the lee of Bernie Island, made the painter fast to some bull kelp and flopped down in the bottom of the boat, completely bushed. About 6 o'clock I roused myself, got something to eat and pulled on down to the village of Port Simpson. This was originally the Hudson's Bay Company's trading post, Fort Simpson, on the Nass River. The name of the trading post was changed to Port Simpson when it moved to this sheltered harbor which already had the name Simpson. For many years it was a favorite place for Alaska Natives to sell their furs and buy British trade goods, despite the efforts of U.S. Customs to stop that traffic.

I debated going ashore in Port Simpson but didn't. I was an alien and had not yet gone through the formalities of entering the country. The Indian village appeared to be down close to the beach, on each side of the wharf, but up on the hill behind them were what looked like regular English estates. I anchored near the wharf for the night.

Wednesday was July 29, my 20th birthday and I spent it rowing along off the coast of part of the Tsimpsean Peninsula, named for the Natives of this part of the country. In the afternoon I passed Old Metlakatla from where, in 1887, many of the residents, followers of Father William Duncan, migrated to Annette Island in southern Alaska. There they formed a new town which they named Metlakatla for their former home.

A short distance past Metlakatla I came up to a boat, the DUNDAS, at anchor. A sign in the rigging said "Buyer" and two men were sitting on deck, enjoying the sun. They said they were waiting for the season to open on the Nass River and would probably tow two or three Metlakatla boats up there. We talked for awhile and they invited me to have supper with them. The boat was nearly as large as the LLOYD C. but there were only two men on it and, of course, no cook. I could not help contrast the meal I had had aboard the LLOYD C. with the one aboard the DUNDAS. It consisted of canned corned beef, sliced as it came out of the can; potatoes boiled with the jackets on and not quite done, peas and carrots that had been heated in the can, and canned peaches for dessert.

It was late evening when I left my hosts and followed a narrow channel into Prince Rupert Harbor. I anchored for the night in a cove opposite the town. Prince Rupert was about the same size as Ketchikan and was also a fishing port. And it was also the western terminus of the Canadian National Railroad and a lot of fish from Alaska were shipped east on the railroad. The railroad in summer ran special fish trains east from Prince Rupert, high-speed trains that had precedence over passenger trains and that stopped only to take on fresh ice to preserve their cargo of fish.

I didn't cross the harbor to the town until 11 o'clock Thursday morning. I would have gone a lot earlier had I known that Thursday afternoons were holidays and everything closed up.

I hunted along the waterfront and found a government float where a small patrol boat was moored. Nobody was aboard to give me permission to tie up there but I did anyway and figured the boat would be fairly safe. By the time I got up town all of the stores and the post office were closed, so I couldn't get mail or buy any stores. Fortunately the customs office was open, so I entered and cleared the boat. To do that I had to fill out about nine different papers in triplicate and that took until the office closed at 4 o'clock and part of the following morning.

The skipper of the patrol boat was aboard when I got back to the float and after he talked with me for awhile he gave me permission to remain there overnight. I ate supper at a restaurant, walked around the business district for a short while and turned in. In the morning I had an early breakfast at the first restaurant I found open. It was run by a Chinaman and it was good. When I finished with the papers at the customs office I was told that my boat would have to be examined and inspected before I could leave. They gave me a list of several officers who could do the inspecting and one of them was the skipper of the patrol boat, a Mr. Stamford.

I hurried back to the float but he wasn't aboard and I chased around town for the next two or three hours trying to find him or another officer on the list. I finally went back to the float and Mr. Stamford was on board. He made a very cursory inspection of the boat and asked whether I had a gun on board. I almost said, "No" before I remembered that my father had given me the .41 Colt revolver he had brought to Alaska with him in 1903. It was wrapped in a piece of oilskin and in the bottom of the grub box. I dug it out and handed it to him.

"I'm supposed to seal this," Mr. Stamford said, "but there's a chance you might need it. If you stop at an Indian village or camp some of those young bucks might get rambunctious, especially with a lone white man." Then he gave me the seal and showed me how to put it on the muzzle of the gun. "Don't use the gun unless you have to," he said, "and I would suggest that you avoid the Indian towns. And be sure to put the seal on before you go to the customs office when you leave Canada." He asked whether I would be stopping at Vancouver and I said it would more likely be Victoria as I planned to follow down the Vancouver Island shore after I went through Seymour Narrows. "Be careful in the narrows," he said. "That's a bad piece of water." Then he wished me good luck and went back up town.

My father had suggested that I visit the American Consul in Prince Rupert and I had been too busy to do so. I was anxious to get away and almost passed up that visit, but decided I should see him. I found his office and that visit changed the whole complexion of the trip. When I left the office I had a companion, although not a female one.

Prince Rupert to Koeye River

The U. S. Consul greeted me warmly and asked what I was doing and where I was going. When he learned that I was going to Puget Sound he said, "Wait here. Don't go away," and ran out.

I looked at some navigation charts he had on the wall and waited a little impatiently for about 15 minutes until he returned. He brought with him a young fellow whom he introduced as Roger Lightoller who had just arrived from Halifax on the train and was looking for a way to get to Vancouver where he had a sister. He had been attempting to work his way to Vancouver in a coasting vessel, but without any luck. The consul wondered whether I might consider taking him with me. Lightoller asked me whether I had a sail and I said I had a small one but I hadn't used it much because I had not had much experience with sail. He said that he had grown up on the coast of England and had spent a lot of time in small sailboats.

That was a factor that helped me decide to invite him to join me. I was behind schedule and it was still a long way to Puget Sound. The days were getting shorter, the more so as I moved south, and that tended to cut down on each day's travel time. Two men rowing could move the boat a little faster, and his sailing experience might also help to move us along. And on top of all that, he was a British subject and that might be handy if we got into trouble and needed some help. So we shook hands on it and he went to collect his gear.

Roger came from a seafaring family. His father had been an engineer in the TITANIC. He was on duty in the engine room when the ship began to sink and was standing under one of the big ventilators that extended to the top deck. The suddenly compressed air in the engine room as the ship sank blew him up the ventilator and into the water where he was pulled aboard a lifeboat.

Roger himself, three years older than I, had just completed an apprenticeship in British tramp steamers and had his papers as an able seaman. He fortunately had a sailor's luggage, everything in a couple of duffel bags which we found room for in the dory.

It was about six o'clock by the time we pulled away from the float at

Prince Rupert and crossed the channel to Digby Island.

The weather had turned misty and foggy and we did not find a camping place. It was getting dark when we reached the wharf and buildings of the Canadian Lighthouse Service. We landed on the beach and went up to the agent's house and he gave us permission to camp on a little patch of grassy ground near the blacksmith shop. We put up the tent, had a mug-up and turned in.

In the morning we unloaded the boat, borrowed a saw and hammer and a few nails from the lighthouse agent and built a sort of locker in the bow and another in the stern to hold food stores and odds and ends. We rearranged everything so we could both row comfortably and managed to get everything stowed so there was still room for one person to sleep. The agent gave us tide and current tables for British Columbia waters and made a list of the lighthouses we would be passing.

It was 1:30 when we got started down the channel behind Ridley Island and Lelu Island. On the shore to our left were the tracks of the Canadian National Railroad and trains were passing frequently. We got a fair wind after a time and sailed most of the way to Inverness which had a salmon cannery and not much else. Roger had never seen one so we went ashore and went through it. It was not running at the moment, having finished for the day.

It was old-fashioned by Alaska cannery standards; they packed the fish in the cans entirely by hand, but did have an iron chink for cleaning the fish and a double-seamer to close the cans. We bought a few things at the cannery store and pulled across the channel to Smith Island and camped for the night.

The next day was Sunday, August 2, and there was no fishing on Sunday, the same as in Alaska. We broke camp and started about noon to cross the mouth of the Skeena which, so far as we could see, is in a deep gorge and had very muddy water. There were canneries scattered along the shore a few hundred yards apart. All afternoon gillnet boats, all of them open boats powered by oars, were going by in the tow of cannery tenders. All were heading up the river. Some of the tenders had as many as twenty boats in tow.

About 3 o'clock we realized that the tide was taking us up the river so we pulled in close to a steep bank and made fast to the limb of a tree to wait for the turn of the tide and watch the boats go by. Fishing would start at 6 o'clock and at that hour several cannon were fired up the river and the fishermen began heaving their nets into the water. The tide turned about then and we cut loose and decided to travel all night. At 10 o'clock we pulled in to a beach on Gibson Island and cooked some supper. We got under way again at 11 and divided the remainder of the night into two watches of about three hours each. One of us rowed while the other slept. I took the first watch and by midnight we were in Grenville Channel, a long, narrow body of water.

For us there was both an advantage and a disadvantage in traveling the narrow channels through British Columbia. The tide was a big advantage. In theory the tidal current would change direction about every six hours, but actually it changed first in the middle of the channel and continued to run in the opposite direction near the shores. It was thus possible to get as much as eight hours of fair tide, although the last part of it was of diminished velocity. In addition, the wind was either fair or dead against you.

The big disadvantage, for us, was the steamboats. We were mostly in the main steamer channels and there was a good deal of traffic. The Canadian National Steamship Company was running three big new passenger boats that summer, the PRINCE ROBERT, PRINCE DAVID and PRINCE HENRY. They were very fast and threw an enormous swell. We didn't want to be too close to them when they passed but we didn't want to be too close to the beach, either. Those waves pounded the shore like ocean surf. There were other steamers, too, but those three were the real wavemakers and we kept close watch whenever we landed to cook. When we camped we looked for an inlet that offered some shelter from that hazard.

After traveling all night we landed behind a little hook of land at 5:30 in the morning of August 3 to cook some breakfast.

Roger, with his sailing experience, was not satisfied with steering with an oar on one side of the boat. We made a rudder out of some driftwood, rigged the sail somewhat differently and took off again at 11 o'clock with a fair wind and tide. We stopped for an hour in Nabannah Bay which isn't much more than an open bight on the east shore of the channel. On the north side of the bight is Morning Point and on the south side is Evening Point and it is about here that the flood tide meets after entering Grenville Channel from the ocean. To here we had done our traveling on the flood but hereafter would do it on the ebb.

Our next stop, at 7:30 that evening, was at Lowe Inlet where there was a cannery and, we had been told, a store. But the cannery was closed and so was the store. The watchman told us of a store near the south end of Grenville Channel but we decided to camp for the night at Lowe Inlet. It was well that we did as there was heavy rain during the night but we were snug enough in the tent.

There was a light mist on the water when we left Lowe Inlet the next morning but it soon cleared away and the sun came out and brought with it a light westerly breeze. We sailed all day, but not terribly fast. In the afternoon we came to a waterfall that fell to the beach just above the high tide line. We landed and stripped down for a wash-up. The water was cold, very cold, but it did carry away some of the grime. We found the bay where there was supposed to be a store but we couldn't find it and at 9 o'clock p.m. stopped for the night inside Promise Island.

The next store was at Butedale and we decided to get there as fast as possible as we were getting short on grub. We got an early start and rowing and sailing crossed Wright Sound to Point Cumming and then through McKay Reach and into Fraser Reach. The latter is less than a mile wide with steep shores and practically no indentations in either of them. We met the PRINCE HENRY and really got tossed by her wake which bounced back from both shores and created something resembling a tide rip.

It was getting dark and we had decided to keep traveling in order to get to Butedale when a fish scouting boat named the JUNE BUG came

The cannery at Butedale in British Columbia.

along and offered us a tow. It was around 9 o'clock when we reached Butedale where there was a cannery, a cold storage and a fertilizer plant. Water from Butedale Lake furnished power for the plants. The store was still open, late as it was, and after we bought some groceries we asked about a camping place. The clerk pointed to a shack across the harbor and we went there. It had the appearance of being lived in but nobody was about. We cooked some supper, made ourselves comfortable and bedded down for the night.

The next morning as we were washing up a little skiff pulled up to the beach and a man with a wooden leg climbed out and came up the beach. He carried a rifle under his arm and leaned heavily on a stout staff. We had some misgivings about the intentions of the new arrival as we had moved in without much formality. Roger whispered to me that the man reminded him of Long John Silver of pirate fame.

We stepped out onto the porch to meet him and apologized for usurping his cabin. "That's all right, you're welcome," he said.

"I thought at first the Indians had moved in." He accepted the cup of tea Roger offered him. His name was MacMillan, "Mac MacMillan," he said. Presumably he had a first name but he did not announce it. We spent the day listening to his stories of hunting and logging and the earlier days in this part of British Columbia, then accepted his hospitality for another night. He wanted us to stay for a week, go hunting with him and then go to a hot springs he knew about somewhere back in the hills.

It was a little after noon when we left Mac MacMillian and Butedale behind and sailed down Graham Reach with a fair wind.

The weather was clear, sunny and warm. We expected to make Swanson Bay for our next stop but MacMillian had told us to be sure to see the salmon going up the falls at Indian River. Near that point we stopped to watch a seiner complete a set, purse up the net and brail it. Roger had never seen a seiner at work and was quite fascinated. We talked to the men on the seiner and learned that the catch was about 3000 fish. They considered it rather poor. A fast little American cruiser that we had seen at Butedale came down the channel while the seiner was brailing and circled around to watch the process.

Because we had spent more than two hours watching the men at work, we hoped we might get a tow to Swanson Bay and went over to the people on the cruiser. We didn't ask for a tow but talked with a man who seemed to be the skipper. After he learned that we were rowing down to Vancouver and Tacoma he said, "Well, I'd offer you a tow only I'm afraid I'd spoil your publicity," and he went inside the cabin and shut the door. That miffed us a little and we probably wouldn't have accepted a tow if he had changed his mind and offered one. By then it was after 6 o'clock and our sailing wind had died, so we made camp a quarter of a mile or so above what we had been told was Indian River although our chart showed it as Canoona River, across the channel from the entrance to Khutze Inlet.

There was a big rock at our campsite and we found some driftwood and part of a fallen tree and built a big fire against the rock. We put some spuds in the fire to roast, then forgot about them until they looked so badly burned that we left them. In the morning, however, after the fire was dead, Roger dug one of them out and cut it open. It was charred for a quarter of an inch or so all around, but the rest was just nicely done, so we hauled them all out and made a breakfast of them.

Roger had never seen salmon fighting their way up over a falls so in the morning we pulled down to the mouth of the river and went up to watch them. They were sockeyes going up to the lake from which the river flows, and there were lots of them. Roger was fascinated and tried to catch one with his hands without, of course, any luck.

By the time we were tired of watching the fish a stiff wind had come up from the south. In addition to being a headwind, it was blowing against the tide and the water was very choppy. We tried rowing against it without making any progress, so we tied up in a kelp patch to wait for the tide to change. After a little while a small trolling boat came chugging and pounding down the channel, not too far off our shore. "Let's try for a tow," I said and got the painter ready. This was 30 feet of one-inch line spliced into the bow of the boat.

The troller was making fairly heavy weather of it and approached slowly. Watching it, the boat seemed to stand still in one spot for several minutes, pounding the waves down flat, then to surge ahead a little way. When it got close we cut loose from the kelp and I rowed out into the channel while Roger held up the painter. The troller stopped close to us and a tall elderly man came on deck. He didn't say a word but held out his hand for the painter which Roger tossed to him. While he was making it fast I yelled that we were going to Swanson Bay. He nodded and went back inside and threw in the clutch. He had not invited us aboard so we both sat back in the stern of the the dory to keep the bow up so it wouldn't sheer.

We didn't travel very fast but it was faster than rowing against that wind. When we got down to Swanson Point, the north point at the entrance to Swanson Bay, the troller pulled over just inside the point. Then he slowed down, came on deck and cast off the painter and started back inside. We yelled our thanks, against the wind. He may have heard because he waved a hand before he went inside .

Swanson Bay was named for the same Captain John Swanson for whom Swanson Harbor, on Icy Strait in Southeastern Alaska, was also named. He had been the skipper of several of the Hudson's Bay Company steamers that had plied the waters of both British Columbia and Southeastern Alaska in earlier years.

I had visited Swanson Bay some years earlier on a small steamer. My father was the Sitka agent for the Border Line Transportation Company which served both British Columbia and Alaska ports with the DESPATCH, ALKI and perhaps others. My mother took my sister and me to Tacoma each year to visit her parents and of course we traveled in Border Line ships in the few years that company operated. It was during the war years, either 1917 or 1918, that we made our visit. The big sawmill was running full blast and what I remembered most clearly was that some of the mill hands wore turbans. I assume they were from India.

The sawmill, or part of it, was still there when we pulled up at a long float, but it was not running and looked pretty dilapidated. There were piles of lumber, however, under some open sheds and there was an agent who ran a small store and handled sales of the lumber. We bought a few things in the store and the agent pointed out a deserted shack we could use if we wanted to stay there overnight.

Two well-maintained houses were occupied by fisheries agents and the pilots of their planes which were out on patrol but would return later in the day. We took some of our gear to the shack and while Roger went off to explore I sat in the dory, got out the typewriter and started a letter. While I was at that the yacht CAROLINE came in and tied up on the other side of the float. She was one of several vessels owned by Campbell Church and used to carry hunters and sports fishermen from Seattle to various places in Alaska.

After a bit a man wearing a yachting cap came across the float and asked if my name was DeArmond. I said that it was. He introduced himself as Casey Moran, the skipper of the CAROLINE.

He said he had read in the Ketchikan Chronicle about my trip and had been keeping an eye out for me. He asked whether I needed anything and I told him that I didn't and that I now had a partner.

I asked Casey that if they went to Sitka to drop in at the post office and tell my mother that he had seen me and that all was well. He said that he didn't think they would make Sitka on this trip but that after leaving Swanson Bay they were going right through to Ketchikan and that he would send a wire to my folks from there. His passengers returned from their inspection of the place about then and the CAROLINE pulled out, northbound.

On Sunday morning, August 9, we had just finished eating breakfast and were packing our gear to the dory when a man stepped off a fisheries patrol boat that had come in during the night. He said he was going down the channel about six miles and would give us a tow if we wished. We did. We weren't overlooking any chances for a lift just for the sake of saying that we had rowed a huge distance. We piled our stuff into the dory in a hurry and he towed us down to Sarah Head, the north end of Sarah Island.

We had a choice at that point, with Hiekish Narrows on the east side of Sarah Island, Tolmie Channel on the west. We picked the latter and hoisted sail. Both wind and tide were fair until the middle of the afternoon when the wind shifted and began to blow from the south. It was very hot and we pulled in behind Tenas Island to make camp. There was a fine display of lightning in the evening and into the night, with loud claps of thunder. By morning it was raining and there was a stiff southerly wind.

We wanted to make Klemtu by that evening and started out when the wind moderated a little at 11 o'clock. It was hard pulling and we were happy when the seiner CAROLINE came along as we were passing Jane Island and offered us a tow. The next island south of Jane Island is shown on the chart as Cone Island but is more often called China Hat because of its resemblance to that style of headgear. The cannery and village at Klemtu are also sometimes called China Hat. Thanks to the CAROLINE we reached Klemtu at 1:30 in the afternoon. The rain had increased to a downpour and the wind had picked up again.

We bought some groceries at the cannery store, then looked for a camping place. There was nothing flat near the cannery so we went across the little bay and found an old blacksmith shop near the shore. The roof was leaking in spots, so we pitched the tent inside to sleep in and brought all of the gear out of the boat and found dry spots for it. A forge stood in one corner of the shop and the blower was still in working order. We cut some wood and built a fire in the forge, then took turns cranking the blower. The fire got really hot and warmed the place up despite some gaps in the walls.

Roger made good use of the forge in another way. The anvil was still there and a couple of hammers as well as a little bit of blacksmith coal. He hunted around and found a couple of old files and forged and hammered them into gaff hooks. We later cut a couple of fairly straight beach alders and lashed the gaff hooks to them. Thus armed, Roger was able to hook out a salmon the next time we came to a spawning stream. He had never seen salmon, or that method of catching any fish, and was delighted.

An Indian village was a short distance south of the blacksmith shop and a cemetery was between the village and the shop and very close to the latter. None of the Indians came near our camp. We scrounged around for firewood which was scarce, but we found a stump, probably hemlock, on the edge of the graveyard. It was out of the ground and the roots had been hacked off. It measured about two feet across on the end where the tree had been cut off and it bulged out from there to nearly three feet and was about three feet high.

The stump did not roll easily but with a good deal of effort we managed to get it down to the shop. Then we set about trying to split it. The small axe we had didn't even faze it and we hunted all around the shop for some kind of a wedge. No luck, so we got a good fire going on the forge, using the last of the coal, and tried to lift the whole stump onto the forge. The two of us together could get it a foot off the ground, but that was all. We gave that up after three failures and tried something else. We thought of using the heavy oars as an incline up to the forge but were afraid they wouldn't hold the weight of the stump. Then we remembered seeing an old boat haulout or gridiron a little distance up the beach and we went out in the pouring rain to look at it.

Most of the timbers had been carried off, probably for firewood, but there was one 6 by 6 about 25 feet long that was sound except for a foot or two at one end. It was waterlogged and too heavy to carry so we got a piece of line from the dory, hitched to one end of the timber and worked up a good sweat dragging it back to the shop. The timber worked like a charm as an incline, although balancing the stump on it and rolling it up toward the forge was tricky. I was reminded of Huck Finn and the grindstone, but neither of us got mashed. We scraped up the last vestiges of coal that was scattered around the dirt floor and managed to set fire to the stump with a lot of help from the blower. It burned very well so long as the blower was going. In fact, the burning stump gave a better light than the coal oil lantern once it got dark and we sat up, reading by its light and taking turns on the blower.

The weather continued bad with lots of wind and some rain on the 12th and we spent another day in camp. It began to moderate on the morning of Thursday, August 13, and we prepared to leave.

The stump was still smoldering on the forge and Roger gave a few turns on the blower as we left the shop. We pulled across to the cannery to pick up a few things at the store, then headed out of the bay and on south. There seemed to be a lot of smoke rising from the vicinity of the blacksmith shop as we passed the point.

"I hope we didn't set fire to the building," I told Roger.

"What I hope is that they don't come after us and arrest us for setting fire to their graveyard," he said.

It was just noon when we left Klemtu. We were about four miles south of Cone Island at 3:30 when a cannery tender came along and offered us a tow. It towed us down to and across Milbanke Sound which is exposed to the ocean and can be a rough piece of water, one of the few places the Inside Passage is so exposed. But it was nearly flat calm as we crossed it and we were happy to have it behind us. The tender dropped us at Idol Point, the north end of Dufferin Island, at 6:30 and went off up a channel to the eastward. We pulled around to a cove in Dundivan Inlet and at 7:45 made camp.

There was thick fog Friday morning. A steamboat passed not too far distant, blowing its whistle. There are a lot of bays and channels in that area and we didn't want to take the wrong one so stayed in camp until the fog thinned enough about noon for us to see some landmarks. We stopped first at New Bella Bella, an Indian village and hospital on Campbell Island, across the channel from Bella Bella and its cannery. We went to the hospital in hope of seeing some of the nurses but the front door was guarded by a pair of Indian men who were not particularly friendly. We gave that up and went into a store. The only thing we needed was some mayonnaise, which we were using instead of butter. The place was deserted. We whistled and called but nobody showed up. The store was large but poorly stocked; lots of shelves but most of them empty or nearly empty. We began looking for mayonnaise. After a bit an Indian woman came in the front door. When she saw us she opened her eyes like saucers, then turned and ran. I know that we looked tough and scruffy but hadn't thought it was as bad as that. After a moment another woman came. We asked her if she was the storekeeper but she didn't seem to know. She just shook her head and perhaps did not understand English. Then we asked for mayonnaise and she didn't even shake her head. She mostly seemed anxious to get us out of there.

So we left and pulled across the channel to Bella Bella and its cannery and a large store. We spent an hour there then sailed down the channel with a light westerly breeze and camped in McLoughlin Bay.

We had been told at Bella Bella that there once had been a Hudson's Bay Company trading post, Fort McLoughlin, at this bay. A log building was still standing but in bad condition and I supposed it was what was left of the fort. Later I learned that the fort, built in 1833, was abandoned 10 years later and the buildings were burned by the Indians. Years later the company built a store there and that may have been what we saw. The bay and fort were named for Dr. John

McLoughlin, long the manager of the Hudson's Bay Company post, Fort Vancouver, on the Columbia River. On the beach was the abandoned hull of a small motor boat, a troller or gillnetter. The name on the bow, in very weathered paint, was CUTTY SARK. Roger was incensed that the name of the famous British clipper ship would appear on this old wreck and suggested burning it. Mindful of the customs officer's counsel regarding the Indians and of the proximity of New Bella Bella, I vetoed that notion.

We had a fair wind on Saturday and sailed down Lama Passage to its juncture with Fisher Channel at Pointer Island. We didn't stop at the Pointer Island Lighthouse but went a mile or so down the shore of Hunter Island and pulled in behind a large rock, bare and almost flat on top. The boat was safe from the waves of passing steamers and we camped on top of the rock where we could watch them pass. A dozen years earlier the passenger steamer MARIPOSA had gone ashore not far south of Pointer Island in a fog. She was salvaged only to become a total loss on an Alaska reef a couple of years later. From our perch on top of the rock we speculated as to just where the ship had struck and where her passengers and crew had camped until rescued.

The MARIPOSA had some fame on the Pacific Coast and in the South Seas. She and a sister ship, the ALAMEDA, each 314 feet in length and with engines of 3,000 horsepower, were built at Philadelphia in 1883 for the Oceanic Steamship Company. They ran opposite each other from San Francisco to Sydney, Australia, via Honolulu, Apia, Papeete and Aukland. Robert Louis Stevenson mentioned the ships in his writings about the South Pacific.

In 1912 both ships were purchased by the Alaska Steamship Company and reconditioned for the Alaska run, usually from Seattle to Seward with stops at other ports between. In October 1915 the MARIPOSA, in command of Captain Charles J. O'Brien, left Seattle and was to go as far as the new town of Anchorage. She carried 70 passengers and a full cargo which was valued at $94,000. In the early morning hours of October 8 the ship struck a rock close to the beach a short distance south of Pointer Island. The passengers were taken ashore in the lifeboats and were later picked up by the steamer DES-PATCH of the Admiral Line and taken to Ketchikan.

The ship was salvaged and repaired, only to end her career on Strait Island Reef near Wrangell in November 1917.

On Sunday, the 16th, we headed for Namu with its cannery and store. It was clear and warm with a light westerly wind blowing down Fisher Channel but it was not strong enough to be worth putting up the sail. As we were coming up to Kisameet Island at the entrance to the bay of the same name we saw a houseboat at anchor in the bay and pulled in to investigate. It proved to be the summer quarters of a man guarding this sockeye stream and lake from poachers. We asked how far it was to the lake and he said it was about a quarter of a mile, with a good trail. Roger asked permission to gaff a couple of salmon and was told he could take two but no more.

We each grabbed a bar of soap and a towel and headed for the lake. It had a gravel bottom, at least near its outlet, and while the water wasn't warm, it wasn't icy cold. We soaked in it for the best part of an hour, crawling out now and then to warm up in the sun. A pair of swans stayed far out on the lake. If they had a nest on shore they didn't go near it while we were there. Roger hooked a salmon and we decided that was all we could use before it spoiled. We were going to build a fire and cook it for dinner but when we got to the beach the stream guard invited us aboard his houseboat for dinner.

During dinner, which was bountiful, he asked us whether we played bridge and we admitted that we played at it. Apparently the only draw-back to his job was the lack of another bridge player and as a result we stayed up most of the night playing three-handed bridge. He was a far better player than either of us but he urged us to stay over another day. We pleaded lack of time, slept for a few hours on the deck of his houseboat and took off after he had fixed us a large breakfast.

We reached Namu, a salmon cannery, general store and oil dock, about 7 p.m. and stayed there overnight. In the morning we got a tow from the boat OGDEN which was taking some people from the pulp mill town of Ocean Falls to join others who were camping at the Koeye

River. Despite the spelling, the residents rendered it "Quay." There was a beautiful little bay at the mouth of the river, with a narrow entrance between two spits of white sand. It was mostly sand around the bay, too. The people arriving on the OGDEN suggested that we might want to stay there, at least overnight, and we decided it was a good suggestion.

With the newcomers there were about 20 people there in four families and with several children. All were from Ocean Falls. We pitched our tent a little distance from their camp so as not to intrude, then went off to explore the river. It apparently drained several lakes and was both wide and deep and had a strong flow of water. We went up it, against a strong current, for a mile or so.

When we got back to the camp a picnic supper was just getting started and we were invited to join the crowd. The centerpiece was an enormous kettle of baked beans with lots of salt pork and ham, and there was plenty of everything else to go with the beans. We had finished eating and were sitting around the fire, talking, when a couple of the women decided to row across the bay. They were not very expert on the oars but were making progress toward the far side of the bay and nobody was paying them much attention until we heard them scream. It was quickly evident that they had been caught by the ebb tide and the current from the river and were being swept out through the narrow entrance and into Fitzhugh Sound. One of the men ran down the beach, shouting at them to pull in to the shore, but they seemed incapable of doing that. So out they went into the sound. There was no power boat and the women had the best skiff. What was left was a canoe and a very small skiff, and our dory. We unloaded everything from the dory except a tow line, declined offers of help and took off after the boaters. Between an ebb tide and a light northerly wind they were a mile or so down the sound by the time we caught up with them.

The two women were frightened almost to the point of hysteria. We took their boat in tow but it was a hard tow with them in it and we discussed taking them aboard the dory but decided against it. The

ery cranky when empty, safe enough but scary when you
sed to it. Neither woman was wearing a life jacket and in
tional condition they seemed safer where they were. So we
he oars. The entire contingent was lined up on the beach,
ng us. We made slow progress until we reached the entrance to
y and there progress almost ceased. Although the tide was start-
flood, most of the current in that narrow entrance came from
t iver.

took at least 15 minutes with both of us pulling on the oars as
hard as we could pull, with the crowd on the spit cheering us on, to
get the two boats through the short entrance. We were a tired pair of
boys by the time we beached the dory.

It was almost dark by then but none of the other people seemed to
be thinking of sleep. They built up a big bonfire and invited us to join
them for some food and word games. We did grab a bite to eat but
begged off the word games and turned in. We wanted to get to
Addenbrook Island by the next night and that meant an early start.
The lighthouse agent at Prince Rupert had especially emphasized
making a stop at the Addenbrook light.

The keeper, he said, was an elderly Scotchman who kept chickens,
lots of chickens. He always had eggs to give away, we were told, and
we didn't want to miss out on that.

Koeye River to Strait of Georgia

The bonfire party must have lasted until late as there was nobody in sight when we rolled out about 7 o'clock, got some breakfast, loaded the dory and went shooting out of the inlet on the current from the Koeye River. It was hazy and warm but there was a moderate and fitful breeze from the north so we alternated between the sail and the oars.

We were about halfway to Addenbrook Island when we were joined by a large whale. I say a large whale, but we did not actually see enough of it to tell how big it was. We had not seen or heard anything of it until it surfaced some 20 feet behind the dory with a loud "whoosh" that was, to say the least, startling.

As it was to windward of us, we received the full benefit of its malodorous breath. After blowing two or three more times, it disappeared. It didn't roll over and throw its flukes in the air like a humpback but simply sank out of sight.

We thought that was the end of that adventure, but we were wrong. Ten or fifteen minutes later it surfaced again, with the same startling "whoosh" and about the same distance astern. We soon learned to grab our noses each time it exhausted its lungs. It followed us, keeping about the same distance astern, whether we were rowing or under sail. Only a part of its head showed, at least from where we were; enough of it that its eyes were just above the surface. We could not see both eyes at the same time but first one eye, then the other, was staring at us. We tried rowing as hard as we could, to get away from the creature, but it stayed just about the same distance behind us. After several minutes of inspecting us, the whale would sink from sight, leaving scarcely a ripple on the water, only to "whoosh" back into view after a short while.

We later learned from the lighthouse keeper that the whale was known to the local fishermen as Billy and that it spent the summers in this area and that it often followed small boats, apparently solely out of curiosity. We got a little but not entirely used to Billy by the time we got to Addenbrook Island.

There was no harbor there for the boat, but there was a crane with a hand-cranked hoist. After receiving permission from the keeper, we fashioned a sling by making the end of the painter fast to a becket in the stern and with a lot of hard cranking we got the dory up to a platform below the lighthouse.

The lighthouse agent had not exaggerated about the chickens on Addenbrook Island, or the light keeper's generosity with eggs. There must have been at least two hundred chickens in a large chickenwire pen which enclosed a large shed for them to roost in and a slightly smaller one equipped with nests. Wires were strung from the sheds to the tops of the posts of the pen and feathers and bits of cloth fluttered from the wire. They were obviously there to frighten away birds of prey and I asked the keeper, whose name was Mac something, whether he was much bothered by predators. He replied but his brogue was thicker than the walls of the lighthouse and I didn't understand more than two out of ten of his words. Roger did better at that than I. He told me that he had had shipmates who used the same brand of what purported to be English.

The keeper may or may not have talked to his chickens but he certainly talked to us non-stop and seemed not to care whether he got any answers. We had rather hoped we might be treated to a chicken dinner but that wasn't to be. Hens apparently were for laying eggs, not for eating. We did have fried eggs for dinner, good fresh eggs and all we wanted of them, but not much of anything else. The keeper didn't offer us beds. Perhaps he had no spares so we camped in a storage shed next to the platform where the dory rested.

The next morning brought fog, low down on the water so that we looked down on it from the lighthouse. We had more fried eggs for breakfast after which we climbed to the top of the lighthouse and watched a couple of steamers go past, one in each direction. We could hear their whistles but all we could see was the tops of their masts as they went tearing along at what appeared to be full speed. That was scary for us. We didn't want to be in the steamboat channel in a fog but weren't sure how to keep out of it.

We had another problem, too. I had lots of equipment but had over-looked including a good boat compass. I had a little Boy Scout compass that was virtually useless in a bobbing boat. This was a place we could have used a good compass, but there was no place we could buy one. The sun finally burned away the fog but it remained hazy and the light keeper told us it was smoke from forest fires farther south. That bothered me some because I had a memory of a forest fire in that area. My mother, sister and I were northbound on one of the steamboats and there was a big fire on each shore of one of the channels. We all had to stay down in the dining room while the ship passed the fires, and the stewards handed out wet wash cloths we could hold over our eyes if the smoke got too thick. We could see the fires through the portholes on each side of the dining room. Up on deck the crew had the fire hoses out, wetting everything down. Apparently the only damage was a little blistered paint. I didn't fancy rowing the boat through that kind of hazard, and it turned out that we didn't have to.

While we were loading our gear into the dory the keeper began loading it with eggs, lots of eggs, boxes and buckets made out of five-gallon coal oil cans. He would have filled the dory if we had let him, insisting that if we couldn't use them we could give them away. When we finally lowered the boat to the water and got started, we rather hoped Billy the whale would show up so we could try him on some surplus eggs. He didn't.

We had to make a choice as we left Addenbrook Island. We could turn eastward toward the mainland or we could cross to Calvert Island and on down to Cape Calvert, its southern tip. We chose that because we thought we would have a better slant of wind across Queen Charlotte Sound. Either way, we had to cross Queen Charlotte; there was no way around it. It was the longest stretch of open water, exposed to the ocean, on the Inside Passage that extends from Puget Sound to Skagway. That can be approximately 50 miles of very rough water, although it can also be like a millpond, as it was when we were crossing it.

It was hot and smoky and almost flat calm as we crossed Fitzhugh

Sound that Thursday, August 19. The sun was blood red and beat down without mercy. As we approached Canoe Cove near the tip of the island a light westerly breeze began to blow. We decided to go into the cove, make a meal of eggs, then, if the breeze held, to push on across the sound during the night.

We had pretty husky appetites when we moved the gasoline stove ashore and set it up to cook some eggs, but we soon lost them. None of the eggs we broke was probably actually rotten but they were very ripe. It became obvious that the Scotchman on Addenbrook Island had unloaded his oldest eggs on a pair of unwary travelers he was unlikely to ever see again. We briefly discussed rowing back to his island and pelting him with some of the eggs, but without any really serious intent.

We finally settled for a kettle of oatmeal which Roger said was known in the British merchant marine as burgoo. That ingested, we dumped the remaining eggs and set sail again. It was getting dark by then and the fog was settling down once more, but we could see Egg Island light as we left the cove and we figured we could hold a reasonably correct course by keeping the wind a couple of points off our stern. The westerly breeze had cleared the air of smoke, which was a relief.

We continued sailing through the night, taking turns sleeping and holding the sheet and tiller. The wind was light but we were moving through the water, although not very fast. Sometime after midnight, listening to the regular whistle signals of a passing steamer, I got the feeling that we were much farther from the steamboat channel than we had aimed to be. I conveyed this feeling to Roger when he woke up and came on watch, but by then the steamer was out of hearing and its signals unavailable for his evaluation. We lamented the lack of a compass, but that was no help, and we agreed to continue steering by the wind.

With daylight the fog thinned a little and the sun rose in the wrong place, directly behind us. The wind had slowly backed during the night, from northwest through north to northeast. We were, in fact, heading directly out to sea. We soon had a landfall where no land ought to be.

My first thought when I saw it was, "Good Lord, we've crossed the Sound and that's the north end of Vancouver Island." Wishful thinking and an impossibility. We would have had to travel at racing speed all night to accomplish that. It turned out to be the south end of Calvert Island, Cape Calvert, which we had left the evening before. We had traveled in a big circle.

It was not only the backing of the wind that fooled us, we learned later. Rivers Inlet and other mainland inlets pour an immense volume of water into Queen Charlotte Sound, especially when the tide is ebbing and this flow continues on through the sound to the ocean.

So we left Cape Calvert behind us again and with both of us rowing. We could see the lighthouse on Egg Island with the Cape Caution area of the mainland behind it. The wind died completely, the sun was merciless and the water was glassy with a long, low ground swell rolling in from the ocean. We wished for a beach umbrella or two for shade but could think of nothing we could rig that would serve the purpose and still allow us to work the oars. So work the oars we did and suffered both from the direct sun and the glare on the water.

The lighthouse keeper on Egg Island didn't have a brogue, didn't keep chickens and was not garrulous, but the few words he did speak made it quite clear that he would be just as happy if we didn't tarry there. So we left and pulled across to the mainland with its many sandy beaches and went into little Indian Cove. This was said to have been a favorite resting place, in early years, for Indian canoes crossing the sound. We would have liked to have camped there overnight but Vancouver and Tacoma were still a long way off and we were behind schedule. We decided to keep traveling.

We cooked a meal, then napped in the shade of a dilapidated shack until the sun was nearly down. Traveling at night, without the bright sun, was much pleasanter and there was no fog that night.

There was no wind, either, unfortunately, and we had to do it all with the oars. At times we both rowed, then took turns on the air mattress. After a time we could see the flash of the Pine Island light near the southern edge of the sound and we headed for it. It was early morning, not quite daylight, when we reached Pine Island and passed inside it. We had decided not to land there but to keep on going. We got a little northerly wind that day and moved down along the Vancouver Island shore and were helped along by the tide in the narrowing channel.

We could see the smoke of a forest fire up ahead and in time we came to the camp of the firefighters in a little cove. Roger thought they might be hiring men, so we pulled in to the camp. The only man in the camp was the cook, who watched us land at a small float and tie up the boat. The first thing he asked was, "Are you hungry?" and of course there was only one answer to that. He fixed us a big meal but was discouraging about the prospect for work on the fire line. He said the fire was mostly contained and only the day before the fire boss had sent three members of his crew down to Campbell River to work on a fire in that area.

We thanked the cook and started off again. I was apprehensive about getting through Seymour Narrows, although they were still some distance ahead. The big tides were coming up and they would be of great help as we moved down narrow Johnstone Strait. That was, of course, long before Ripple Rock had been blasted out of the channel and the narrows with its currents up to 12 knots and enormous whirlpools had a fearsome reputation.

While we were discussing whether to tackle Seymour or to try one of the smaller waterways to the east of it, our problem was solved. A big steam tug, the R.F.M., came along towing two barges loaded with lime rock. He was not going very fast and we pulled over close to his course. When a man stuck his head out the wheelhouse window we asked if it would be all right for us to hook on. We couldn't make out his answer because he didn't take his pipe out of his mouth but we took it to be in the affirmative because he didn't shake his head.

When the second barge came along we pulled in behind it. There was a deck about six feet wide at the rear end of the barge and it had about six inches of freeboard. We pulled the bow of the dory up on the deck and made it fast, then unloaded some of our gear and took

Two lime rock barges with the tug far ahead.

My shipmate, Roger Lightoller, on the lime rock barge.

stock. We had enough food of one kind and another for several days but we were short of water. My five-gallon keg had only about a gallon of water in it when we left Canoe Cove to cross Queen Charlotte Sound, and we had used most of that.

"I'll take the keg and row up to the tug and get it filled," I said. Roger was dubious. "I believe we're going a lot faster than you think," he said. "He probably slowed down a lot so we could get aboard." I wasn't convinced. "Two of us could do it easily," I said.

Roger proposed that we try something first. I had a hundred feet of half-inch line and we tied one end of it to the end of the painter and the other end to a bollard on the barge. I got in the dory and shoved off and Roger paid out the line as far as it would go. I swung out to one side, out of the wake, then pulled on the oars as hard as I could pull. I was able to take a little slack out of the line and had perhaps gained ten feet by the time I was exhausted. I felt a bit sheepish as Roger hauled the dory back to the barge and I got out. I admitted that he was a far better judge of speed than I.

So we toughed it out, mighty dry. I think we each had about a cup of water during the thirty-six hours we were on the barge. We passed some small settlements and, of course, many streams and small waterfalls, all of which were extremely tempting. But we resisted. We were bowling along at a great rate, without any effort on our part and would soon be through Seymour Narrows. There wasn't room to pitch the tent but we rigged a tarpaulin to give us some shade, got out of the sun and tried to think cool thoughts. Mostly, however, we caught up on sleep.

We went through Seymour Narrows at night and were both sound asleep. We did take the precaution of sleeping in the dory. "If something happened to this barge, it would go down like one of those rocks it's carrying, and we probably wouldn't wake up until we were floundering in the cold water," Roger said. I took his advice without argument.

After we were out of Seymour Narrows and into the Strait of Georgia the tug turned eastward past Cape Mudge and then southward.

The navigation was being taken care of by others. The weather continued warm, even hot, but atmosphere was hazy and the shores were distant and uninteresting. We slept and talked, and thought about water. We had just turned out about six o'clock in the morning and were still about half asleep when an outboard motor boat came alongside. It was the lifeboat from the tug and aboard it were the captain and a crew member.

The skipper asked us where we were going and when we told him he said they were heading for a pulp mill on the mainland and didn't want to take us out of our way. He suggested we take our leave there and said he would slow down so we could get off safely. We asked whether he could spare us a little water and he took our keg and headed back to the tug. By the time he returned the tug had slowed to bare steerage way and we had the dory loaded. We took the keg and cut loose after thanking the skipper.

Our first order of business was to broach the keg. I poured one of our white enamelware mugs full for Roger and the water was about the color of tea. My first thought was that it had come out of the bilge but Roger recognized it as the product of the engine room condenser. It had been through the engine several times in the form of steam and was barely drinkable. With our thirst we must have downed a quart apiece as we pulled for the nearest shore in search of potable water and a place to cook breakfast.

Vancouver, Bellingham, Tacoma

We were beginning to want to get to Vancouver, didn't get much sailing wind and rowed steadily, going ashore only now and then to cook a meal. At daylight one morning we were approaching a place shown on the map as Hood Bay. The tide was low and we came to a long, flat beach. It looked to be a hundred yards or more from the water's edge to a strip of grass and shrubbery and beyond that were two or three houses.

We piled ashore, set up the gasoline stove and put a pot of oatmeal on one burner and began toasting some bread on the other. We were paying no attention to the upland area until suddenly we heard a woman's voice from that direction: "I say there, what are you doing here? This is private property and you must leave at once."

We looked up to see an imposing dowager. She was wearing what were probably leather riding boots and she carried a riding crop, perhaps for protection. I was too astonished to think of a reply, never having been ordered off a beach before, but Roger took over. Assuming a Cockney accent which I won't try to render in print, he said something on this order: "Begging your pardon, your ladyship, but you see we are just shipwrecked sailors trying to get back to civilization. We are just getting ourselves a wee bite of breakfast and haven't even touched a cockle on your beautiful beach."

She was totally unimpressed. "If you are not gone in ten minutes, I shall call the police," she said and stalked off toward the nearest house.

Roger shrugged. "We must be getting back to civilization," he said. "I doubt she'll call the police, but if she does they probably will show more human kindness than she does."

We took our time finishing our breakfast and finally left without ever seeing a policeman. We rowed to Horseshoe Bay and in a little store there bought oranges, apples and some other supplies. We no doubt could have found a camping place at Horseshoe Bay and we were tempted because we were both tired and short of sleep. But we were also anxious to get to Vancouver and decided to get right along.

We hoped to reach Point Atkinson, at the entrance to Burrard Inlet, on which the city of Vancouver is located, and we both pulled on the oars. There seemed to be an interminable number of points of land between Horseshoe Bay and Point Atkinson but we did reach the point and its lighthouse late in the afternoon and decided to stay overnight in that vicinity. The entrance to Vancouver Harbor, known as Lions Gate, is narrow with strong tidal currents and we weren't sure of the time of slack water. So we consulted the lighthouse keeper and he advised against trying to get into the harbor that evening. We asked and received permission to pitch our tent on the grounds of the lighthouse and got a good sleep for the first time in several days.

When we started out the next morning the wind was just a little too much on the bow for sailing, and it kept rising until it was almost too strong to buck. We pulled into a cove named West Bay and waited for it to calm down. While we were there I remembered that I would have to report to customs, so I got out the revolver and fastened the seal as instructed by the officer in Prince Rupert. Then I wrapped it up again and stowed it away. The wind died in the afternoon, the tide was flooding and we went shooting through Lions Gate like an express train. A float house with a big sign, customs, was anchored in the harbor and we went there. They were not much interested in us at that point but directed us to the immigration dock and float. I was warned, however, to stop at the customs float and formally clear for Bellingham before leaving.

It was different at the immigration office. The man there took one glance at Roger's passport and waved him on. So far as I could see he didn't even write down the name. But it was different for me. He had a lot of questions: Where did I come from? Why had I not gone through immigration in Prince Rupert? How long was I going to stay in Canada? And so forth. I displayed the paper showing that I had entered customs at Prince Rupert and said I would be leaving for Bellingham as soon as possible. I had to fill out and sign some papers, after which I was granted permission to leave the dory at their float overnight and was told it would be perfectly safe there.

Roger took his duffel bags and I took some things in my pockets and we looked for a place to spend the night. A small hotel near the waterfront seemed to be the answer, but that was a mistake. What we each wanted, as much as anything, was a bath but after we had paid our money we discovered that while it had toilet facilities it had neither a tub nor a shower. We were too tired to hunt up another place and probably could not have gotten our money back anyway.

We parted company in the morning. Roger set out to find his sister's house but we intended to keep in touch so I got her address. And, by good fortune, I also asked him for her telephone number. I then set out for the waterfront in hope of catching the last of the ebb through Lions Gate. That was not to be.

When I walked down the gangway to the float at the immigration Dock, I noticed a member of the Northwest Mounted Police, in full uniform, standing near my boat. I said, "Good morning," and started to untie the painter.

"Wait a minute," the policeman said. "I have some questions to ask you." I immediately thought of the revolver. The man at the customs float had not asked about guns and I had not thought to mention it to him. But it wasn't that.

"You came from Alaska?" the officer said, a combination statement and question. I said that was true. "You stopped at Prince Rupert?" I said I had. "And at Prince Rupert you took aboard another man, a British subject?" I said that was true, and gave him Roger's name. "Where is he now? What did you do with him?" the policeman wanted to know. I explained that I had left him only a few minutes earlier and that he was on his way to his sister's house, which I understood was in West Vancouver.

The Mountie took me up to the immigration office, but neither of the men on duty there had been there the day before when I checked in and so were of no help to me. There was no record that Roger had been there. I suggested that the Mountie call the sister's number and he did and talked with the sister who apparently told him that she had heard nothing from her brother and didn't know where he was, but that she was expecting him sometime. That seemed to make him even more suspicious.

"You stay right here until I come back," he said. I asked whether I could go down to my boat but he vetoed that and left. I asked one of the immigration officers if he had something I could read and he produced a couple of Vancouver newspapers. I finished them in an hour or so and asked the officer what he thought would happen if I just got in the boat and pulled out.

"I wouldn't advise it," he said. "Those fellows have the 'Get Your Man' attitude and they'd have a patrol boat or two after you in no time. You wouldn't get out of the inlet."

So I sat and seethed until the Mountie returned. "OK, you can go now," he said very curtly, with no further explanation. He didn't volunteer to return the paper with the address and phone number on it and I got it only by asking for it.

The tide had turned and the current was too strong for me to get through the narrows. I tried on the Stanley Park side, thinking there might be an eddy there. I couldn't find one, so I drifted back into the harbor and crossed to the north side and tried it there with no better luck. I made fast to a piling and waited, thinking mean thoughts about the RCMP.

It was late afternoon by the time I got past Lions Gate and I decided to keep on going through the night. I wanted to get out of Canada as fast as possible. The lights of the city were on my left and to the right and ahead were the lights of vessels and navigation lights. Off my starboard bow, too, there was a glow on the high clouds that I took to be the reflection of the lights of Victoria.

I knew that the Fraser River had an extensive delta, but I had no idea of its total extent. It did seem to me that the lights I could see on shore were getting very far away and I finally stuck an oar down to take a sounding and found I was in only three feet of water. Soon after that there was only two feet of water and I changed my course more to the west. Soon after that I began to see many lights that seemed to be standing still and were down close to the water. I was puzzled for a time but finally figured out that they were gillnetters with their nets out. Each boat showed a light and there was another light on a buoy at the end of the net which, at a guess, was a thousand feet long. Most of the lights were outside of me, but I did pass inside a couple of boats whose nets stretched out toward the west.

After a time I saw two lights dead ahead but could not determine which was the boat and which the buoy. I pushed ahead slowly, keeping watch for the net and finally came up to the cork line. It probably would have been no problem to go right across it but I decided that was probably poor etiquette and turned toward one of the lights. It proved to be the buoy and I went around it. I was barely past it when there was the crack of a .22 rifle from the direction of the boat and a bullet whizzed by not too far over my head.

That annoyed me after I had taken the trouble to row around his buoy and I wasn't too happy with the Canadians anyway after my experience with the Mountie. I dug out the .41 Colt revolver, tore the seal off, found a cartridge and sent a bullet upward at a high angle. After a bit there was a satisfactory echo from something on shore, but never a sound from the gillnetter. The war was over and I went on my way.

A breeze came up from the north soon after that and I sailed until about 2 in the morning when the wind died. A light fog had come up, I could see no lights or landmarks although I could hear an occasional diesel engine in the distance. I wasn't sure whether I had crossed the boundary but was too tired to really care. I hung the anchor out on about 10 feet of chain so I wouldn't drift ashore, lighted the kerosene lantern and hung it on the mast, and turned in.

When I woke up it was daylight and the dory was bouncing around like a cork. My first thought was that I had drifted into some tide rips although I had not heard of any in this area. Then I heard diesel engines and some voices and I realized that the commotion came from the wakes of a number of boats. One of the voices said, "Somebody must have got drownded out of that boat" and another said, "Maybe there's a dead man under that canvas."

When I poked my head up above the gunwale I realized I was in the middle of the American salmon seining fleet and had crossed the boundary. There were at least a hundred boats, perhaps more. Most of them were big boats, bigger than the Alaska limit seiners; more on the order of the herring seiners that came to Alaska each summer. There can't have been many fish because so many of the boats came charging up close to the dory and stopped to ask who, what, why and how. The dory rocked wildly each time a seiner came close and I didn't dare light the gasoline stove. So I pieced together a cold breakfast and ate it while answering their questions. They didn't seem to have anything else to do. I asked one of them why they didn't go catch some fish and he said they were waiting for the opening after a closed period. Not one of them offered me so much as a cup of coffee.

After I got out the oars and started on my way they let me alone and I headed off in the general direction of Bellingham. There was still limited visibility because of the fog. After a couple of hours I saw a big steam tug coming up behind me. When it was nearly abeam and a couple of hundred yards outside me it swung over in my direction. I could make out the name REDONDO on the bow and, soon afterward, a shield with the letters PAF on the funnel. So it was a tender for Pacific American Fisheries which had its headquarters and a big cannery at Bellingham. The company also had many canneries in Alaska.

The REDONDO slowed down and stopped close to me and a man stepped out of the wheelhouse. "Are you DeArmond?" he asked. I said I was and he said, "I've been watching for you and when I saw the dory I was pretty sure it would be you. Why don't you come aboard and give the oars a rest?"

I didn't need a second invitation, and I didn't deny it when the cook suggested I might be ready for a mug-up. The mug-up amounted to a full breakfast and a hearty one. The skipper, whose name was Johnson, turned the wheel over to someone else and drank coffee while I ate and told about my trip. Many years earlier he had been the deckhand on the MINNIE, a tender for the Ford Arm cannery north of Sitka and he knew many Sitka people and asked about them. It was a pleasant visit and enjoyable ride to Bellingham.

The REDONDO tied up at the cannery wharf in South Bellingham and I got permission to put the dory inside a small float on one side of the cannery. I used a phone in the office to call Dorothy Goddard Wright and a short while later her husband, Don, came and picked me up. Dorothy, a daughter of the Sitka Hot Springs family, had lived with us in Sitka while she was attending school and had baby-sat my sister and me. Later we had spent a week or more at the hot springs each summer while Dorothy was living there.

I stayed overnight with Don and Dorothy but they had a very small house and it was not very convenient for them. The next day I moved, at their invitation, to the home Mr. and Mrs. Fred Miller, the parents of Mabel Miller, my Sitka schoolteacher friend. She had been there for the summer and had left for Sitka just five days before I arrived, but they had been expecting me. They had a big old house and only one daughter, Edith, was still at home.

I stayed over an extra day at the Millers. He was retired but wrote a column twice a week for the Bellingham paper on "general subjects." That apparently covered anything he was interested in, and he was interested in almost everything under the sun. He wanted to know all about my trip and a lot of things about Alaska, and he wanted fish stories, bear stories and shipwreck stories, among others.

It was after noon on Monday, August 31, when I finally got away from Bellingham. It was overcast and there was some fog which grew thicker as the afternoon wore on. It also began to sprinkle and then to pour down rain with a light southerly wind, a head wind for me. It wasn't a good day to travel but I kept pulling on the oar handles.

I had not bothered to get a detailed chart of those waters; I didn't believe I needed one. That was an error. The chart I had covered the entire coast of Washington as well as Puget Sound and the area I needed to know about right then covered very little of the chart. It showed two bays south of Bellingham: Samish Bay and Padilla Bay. The north entrance to Swinomish Slough, which separated Fidalgo Island from the mainland, was in the corner of Padilla Bay and I didn't expect there would be any problem finding it. I was wrong. I wanted to go through the slough rather than around Fidalgo Island and then through Deception Pass to get inside Whidbey Island. There were strong currents in Deception Pass, although probably nothing worse than ones I had encountered farther north.

What the chart did not show, or at least I did not see, was a cove just south of Bellingham. The yacht club was located there and as I passed it I saw the boats. I ticked it off as Samish Bay and kept going. When I entered the actual Samish Bay I thought I was in Padilla Bay and began hunting for the entrance to the slough. It wasn't where I thought it should be, according to the chart. I tried to go ashore to find someone to ask, but the tide was out and there was mud, deep mud, every place I tried. I put on my hip boots to try to wade ashore but the mud was too soft and deep. The tide was falling and after a time I got aground.

There wasn't much I could do except huddle there in my oilskins, back to the wind, and wait for the water to come up again. The rain continued to fall and the fog was as thick as ever. I couldn't see any landmarks or anything else, and what I could hear didn't help any. The railroad tracks ran along the shore there and every now and then a train clattered by. Some of them blew their whistles and that was the only sound of civilization. I could not, however, see the lights of the trains through the fog. I began to feel that I might be there on that mud flat forever.

The tide eventually did come up enough to float the dory and I pulled out to deeper water. It was dark by then as well as foggy and I found a small float house on logs; found it by bumping squarely into it, hard enough that it tumbled me backward off the thwart. I had not expected anything of the kind there. The side of the house that I rammed had a window but no light showed in it and there was no answer when I shouted a greeting. I climbed onto a narrow deck at one end of the raft, carrying my flashlight, and knocked on the door. There was no answer so I tried the door. It was not locked and I entered. It was a single room and did not appear to be lived in. There was no stove or furniture, only a couple of rolled up mats in one corner. On them were a couple of newspapers printed in Oriental characters. It dawned on me then that the float house probably belonged to oyster farmers, Japanese oyster farmers.

I debated for a long time whether to camp there in the house for the night, but I had had no experience with Japanese people and was not sure how they would react to finding a total stranger on their property. So I pulled off a way, dropped the anchor and bedded down in the bottom of the dory for the night. It was far and away the low point of the entire trip. It continued to rain and rain hard. The tarpaulin shed some of it overboard, but by no means all of it. I turned in all standing, including oilskins and boots and had no trouble going to sleep. The trouble was that after a time the water got deep enough that it began to run in my mouth and nose. That woke me up enough to bail it out, or most of it. The whole thing was nightmarish and seemed endless, but it finally began to get light and I shivered awake.

The rain had not stopped but the fog had mostly cleared away. I could see a headland that, after I pulled the chart out of its watertight case, I figured out must be Williams Point, between Samish Bay and Padilla Bay. The float house was not far away but there was nobody around it and I realized that I could just as well have slept there. I opened a can of bully beef and made a cold breakfast of that and some soggy crackers before getting under way.

The weather continued to improve and once I got into Padilla Bay I could see boats going into and coming out of Swinomish Slough. LaConner, when I got there, was a picturesque little town on the mainland side of the slough. I found a sign that said "Barber Baths," got a hot bath that took some of the remaining chill out of my bones and got into some dry clothes. I didn't tarry in the town but bought a few groceries and moved on. That was Thursday, September 3, and I was going to have to keep moving if I was going to make Tacoma by Labor Day.

The good weather didn't last and I had no more than pulled out of Swinomish Slough than the rain started again. Hard rain. The Tacoma paper reported that it rained 2.06 inches in 24 hours there. And with the rain there was wind, a headwind for me. I went down between Camaano Island and the mainland and made very slow progress. That day and the next at least 20 big seine boats passed me but none would take the tow line I waved at them. They weren't fishing, either, just heading for Everett or Seattle. Finally a cannery tender came along towing an empty fish scow and I hailed him. He was going to a cannery just north of Everett and we reached it just about dark on Saturday.

It was still raining and blowing when I reached Edmonds Sunday morning and I decided that I'd had enough. I found a boathouse and the man running it said I could leave the boat there overnight for four bits. He was just cooking breakfast and invited me to join him. After downing three eggs, a lot of bacon and three cups of coffee I felt a hundred per cent better. He surely didn't make any money on that deal.

I started out to find a cheap hotel but stopped to watch a couple of young fellows who were putting an automobile engine into a boat. They seemed to know a lot about engines but very little about boats, and as the rain had ceased, I stopped to help them. It took all day to get the job done and one of the boys invited me and the other fellow to his home for dinner and the other one offered to put me up for the night in his apartment over the garage where he worked.

By Monday morning the weather had cleared and the wind was from the north. I spread the sail and coasted past the northern suburbs of Seattle. I dodged a Bremerton ferry and a couple of other vessels and edged over to go down the west side of Vashon Island. That was somewhat familiar country. A year and a half earlier when I was a senior at Stadium High School in Tacoma I had gone out to Point Defiance Park one fine morning during spring vacation and rented one of the park's rowboats. I had not touched an oar since the previous summer, it was an easy-rowing boat and it felt good to get out on the water. I went up the west side of Vashon Island with a fair tide and almost before I knew it I was at the north tip of the island.

I decided to go on to the eastward because I thought I could portage the boat across a narrow isthmus and put it in the water again in Quartermaster Harbor. When I got there, however, I found that the isthmus was wider than I had thought and there was no way I could drag the boat across. So I bought a couple of sandwiches at a little shop there and decided to go on around the island. It was a lot farther than I realized and the upshot was that I got back to Point Defiance at 1 o'clock the next morning, just in time to catch the last street car to my boarding house. I had a lot of blisters and during the rest of the spring vacation I had difficulty opening my hands fully. I later measured it on the map and I believe the distance is 43 miles. That beat anything I did with the dory, but the park boat was a lot easier rowing.

It was well dark when I reached the north end of Vashon Island with the dory a year and a half later and I was rowing with the last of the flood tide. The tide carried me over to the west side of the channel and at 2 o'clock the ebb had gotten strong enough that I was making no progress. Some of the lights of Tacoma were in sight as I pulled close to shore and dropped the anchor.

I started on again at 5 when the tide had turned. It was my intention to land at the Tacoma Yacht Club but again the tide took charge.

A friend at Bellingham braves the dory.

I did not start soon enough to row across the current toward Point Defiance and had to land at Salmon Beach, a small settlement south of the point. I called Herb Arntson, who had been at Stadium High School when I was, and he picked me up with a car. His older brother, Fred, had gone from Tacoma to Sitka with me during a couple of summer vacations and I had been invited to stay with them while in Tacoma.

I had a bath at the Arntson home, then called Dr. E. A. Rich. Both he and his wife had attended college in Minnesota with my mother. He was an orthopedic surgeon and had patched me up after my encounter with the wrong end of a shotgun some years earlier.

Dr. Rich was also an officer of the Tacoma Yacht Club and we agreed that I would be at the club at 4 o'clock. He then called the News-Tribune and got them to send a reporter and a photographer to the yacht club at 4 o'clock. The result was a long story and a photograph in the News-Tribune the following day. And that story had another result. The reporter was thorough. Among other things, he wrote that I was staying with the Arntson family on North Junette Street. And that evening I had a telephone call from Dale Burlison. She told me some time later that she had called on a dare from a girl friend. We had been in a biology class at Stadium when I was a senior and she was a sophomore and I had helped her dissect a frog or other kind of creature. We had gone to a football game or two and a basketball game, but so far as I can remember those were our only dates. I did remember her but not much more than that.

We agreed to meet at The Cave, a fountain and teen-age hangout in downtown Tacoma, and spent some time together before I went on to Eugene, Oregon, to college. I visited her in Tacoma at Christmas and again the next spring before I returned north. While I was in Eugene and later in Sitka we carried on a rather intensive correspondence.

As a final result of all that, as I write this we are about to celebrate our sixty-third wedding anniversary. For that reason, if for no other, the dory trip from Sitka to Tacoma in the summer of 1931 can be called a complete success.